Bears in the Basement, Raccoons in the Kitchen

CONFESSIONS OF A WILDLIFE BIOLOGIST

WILLIAM E. VANSCOY

PAGE PUBLISHING, INC.
Conneaut Lake, PA

First originally published by Page Publishing 2021

ISBN 978-1-6624-1515-9 (pbk)
ISBN 978-1-6624-1516-6 (digital)

Printed in the United States of America

FOREWORD

MY CHILDHOOD HOME was a zoo. Usually this is meant metaphorically, but in my case, it is literally true. For almost all my childhood I lived in a state-owned house on French Creek Game Farm. When I was three years old, my father became the superintendent of the game farm and held that position until he retired in 2001. He was born and raised on a small West Virginia farm though his farm was more of the cows and chickens variety rather than the black bears and bobcats of my childhood.

In rural West Virginia (WV), he developed a lifelong love of the outdoors and honed hunting and fishing skills that afforded time outdoors and helped put food on the family table. It is fitting that he would become a wildlife biologist.

His education at Ohio State University was supplemented by Army ROTC, and courtesy of Uncle Sam, he resided briefly in Kentucky and South Carolina, where I was born on the day he received his orders for Vietnam. After returning home safely from this tour of duty, it was an easy decision to return to his native West Virginia to work for the Department of Natural Resources. His initial job was working on the Monongahela National Forest, followed shortly thereafter by the game farm superintendent position.

When we first moved to the game farm in French Creek, West Virginia, the facility was little more than a collection of old cages housing a variety of animals indigenous to the state, such as black bears, deer, mountain lions, and turkeys. This new "home" would afford us the opportunity to make many new friends, both of the human and animal variety. The men who worked for my father were a colorful cast of characters, many of whom had unexpected talents. There was the game farm employee who painted the outline of a deer head on my soon-to-be bedroom wall while cleaning his paintbrushes.

The quite lifelike drawing, to my dismay, did not get to stay, but the artist, who had a quick wit and an affinity for pranks that kept his colleagues constantly on their toes, would work at the game farm for several years. Another employee, with no formal music education, could play a mean banjo. There was the veterinarian who usually made his rounds at the game farm around lunchtime, when he could join my family for a meal and often a big slice of homemade pie. A gruff character who quite preferred big, wild animals to the domesticated cats and dogs of his office practice, he became my father's best friend and lifelong hunting buddy. The animal friends were equally surprising. There was the wild boar who spent most of his time sleeping but who would rise and run to the fence when he heard us calling out "pig, pig, pig." My favorite was the big old black bear, Jack, who lived in a concrete-floored cage and routinely feasted on peanuts and soda pop fed to him through his cage by tourists.

To me, the most memorable aspect of growing up at the game farm was that this facility cared for all the orphan animals from around the state. Some of the mothers of these babies had been killed in car accidents or sometimes the babies were found in the woods by well-meaning outdoor enthusiasts who didn't realize that the mothers were just a short distance away. The babies were brought to the game farm to be rescued so spring and summer were frequently busy times of the year for my father, as he ran what amounted to a side gig as an animal orphanage. Over the years there had been fawns, baby bobcats, owls, foxes, and (my personal favorite) black bears, to name a few. Like humans, these baby mammals would feed on milk from their mothers. But in the absence of the mothers, they were bottle-fed by my father's employees, by the occasional WVU student hired for a summer job, and by my family. I can still smell the powdered milk and see the stacks of bottles and nipples used to feed the army of fawns housed every summer in an enclosure a few hundred yards behind our house. I can still feel the thick, wiry fur of a baby black bear and remember how their upper lip would stick out to warn that you might soon get bitten if you weren't cautious. The smallest and most vulnerable of these baby animals were kept inside until they were big and strong enough to be in outdoor enclosures. We sometimes housed orphaned baby black bears in cardboard boxes in our basement, and my father, who reportedly never heard the nighttime cries of his two daughters, was quick to awaken to feed the lonely, crying bear a warm bottle of formula in the middle of the night.

My father's tenure at the game farm was marked not only by development of lifelong friendships and foster parenting of a host of infant wildlife, but more importantly, by a vision of conservation of the natural resources of our beautiful state and of education for its human inhabitants and visitors. This vision included creation of the National Hunting and Fishing Day Celebration, an annual festival celebrating WV's outdoor traditions of hunting and fishing. It was a venue to display campers, equipment, clothing, and demonstrations of the difficult skills of marksmanship, archery, bird dog training, and decoy carving, to name a few. My father also oversaw the transformation of the game farm into the West Virginia State Wildlife Center, ridding the facility of the concrete-floored cages of old and moving the animals into new, natural habitats. He watched as some inhabitants of the facility stepped on grass for the very first time. He led countless tours for schoolchildren over the years, teaching them about the wildlife of their state and their habitats.

I haven't lived in West Virginia since I left home for college, and I have heard far more WV hillbilly jokes than I care to remember. I have read articles and books about the poverty of my home state, the destruction caused by coal mining, the desperation of so many of its people. And yet I was blessed with a truly unique and magical childhood in this poorest of states which, to me, is a place of beauty. Many of the hillbillies of my childhood were smart, talented people who loved nature and wildlife. Few of them had material wealth, but they lived a rich life. I am thrilled that my father has chosen to share a story which gives the reader a different view of this complicated state. This is my father's story of growing up in Appalachia, of honing a love of the natural world and its inhabitants, of being a lifelong hunter and fisherman, of serving as zookeeper and as caregiver to countless orphaned wild animals, and of turning a ramshackle zoo into the wildlife center and conservation facility that it is today. The West Virginia wilderness of my father's childhood has changed dramatically with loss of unspoiled habitat and wildlife that was once abundant—a result of overuse, pollution, carelessness, and climate change. I hope that this memoir will be a reminder of what once was, both in terms of rural lifestyle and of our environment, of the breadth of our natural resources, and of how much these resources deserve our care and protection.

Lori Vanscoy, MD

CHAPTER 1

The Setting

BENJAMIN FRANKLIN ONCE said, "Only two things are certain in life: death and taxes."

Perhaps Mr. Franklin should have added one more certainty: change. No matter what the current circumstances may be, they are certainly going to change.

When Europeans first penetrated the Appalachians, it was said that a squirrel could travel from the Potomac River to the Ohio River without ever having to touch the ground. Pristine, mature forest formed an unbroken canopy. At the higher elevations, most of the forest was composed of black spruce, hemlock, northern red oak, and wild cherry. Lower elevations were dominated by white and red oaks, beech, hickory, tulip poplar, elm, and of course, American chestnut. The variety of tree species in southern Appalachia is contested by only a very few places in the world. While it must have been awe-inspiring to walk through these forests, all these trees were considered a liability by early settlers who wanted to graze cattle and sheep, raise crops, and provide for their families. And so, little by little, the forest was cleared and change began.

Bobcats, wolves, and elk were among the many species encountered by the first European settlers who came into the Appalachian Mountains.
Photos by Steven Rotsch

One might think that such a pristine forest would be teeming with wild game. Such was not the case. Although bison, elk, white-tailed deer, black bears, mountain lions, and wolves did live here, they were not abundant because their ideal habitat was limited by solid canopy forest. Squirrels and wild turkeys did prosper in this habitat because it was much more suitable for them. It is interesting to note that the mixed hardwood forest produced enough mast to attract millions of migrating passenger pigeons whose numbers darkened the daytime sky and whose combined wingbeats could be heard from a mile away. I wish I could have seen that!

By the late nineteenth and early twentieth centuries, much of that forest had been cleared.

Topographic maps of that time revealed that most of the land was pasture, meadow, or crop field. Although it wasn't good crop land, it was believed that corn, wheat, barley, and oats were necessary to sustain a family on a farm.

In the 1920s and 1930s, much of West Virginia was covered by small family farms where it was advantageous to have several children who could help with all the work, and there was plenty of hard work to do. Harvesting hay, corn, grain, and fruit by hand was a slow process. Tending livestock, butchering, and preserving the meat were demanding and detailed jobs. Planting and tending a vegetable garden were work for the entire family, and the process of preserving and storing food for the winter occupied most of the summer and early fall. Also, there was the never-ending requirement of cutting and splitting firewood for cooking and heating the house. By the 1940s, most of those children had grown up, gone off to war or to the cities to participate in the war effort. Once they had seen the world, very few were inclined to return to a hillside farm where it was hard to make a living. Mom and Pop stayed on the farm, but as the years went by, they were less and less capable of doing all that work. Mother Nature stepped in and began the process of reclaiming the forests.

Little by little, the agents of nature—wind, water, birds and animals—began the regeneration of forest. It started around the edges of fields and fence rows, and within a few years, what had once been a grassy meadow became a sapling thicket destined to become a mature forest of saw logs. The face of the ancient Appalachian Mountains and hills was changing right before our eyes, and most of us, because of ignorance of inattentiveness, did not even notice.

I grew up in a small town in a small county in a small state. World War II had just ended, many thousands of servicemen were returning home from overseas, the economy was poised to grow rapidly, and the certainty of change was in the air.

This was the world as I saw it in 1949 and 1950. It was peaceful and quiet. Almost everyone in town knew everyone else. Any misbehavior was quickly corrected by Mom or Dad, either your own or someone else's! Nobody locked their doors at night. Nobody had a television. Only a few families had a telephone and a car, but nobody had two cars. Computers had not yet been invented, and a handheld device was a hammer, pliers, or an eggbeater.

Doctors, clergy, schoolteachers, law enforcement officers, even volunteer firemen were icons in the community, and their work was respected. Their opinions were sought and carefully considered, and their contributions were recognized and appreciated. Sometimes even politicians could disagree in a civil and friendly manner.

Most families had members who hunted, and since wild game belonged to everyone, it could be pursued in season wherever it could be found. It was generally understood that each hunter accepted responsibility for his own person and for his own actions. The specters of paranoia, liability, and litigation had not yet raised their ugly heads, and most could enjoy their sport just about anywhere they wanted. Of course, contact with the landowners and common courtesy were expected, but Posted or No Hunting signs were rare.

This was where I began to really notice the world around me. I began to read books, to watch, to listen, and to wonder.

In 1947 Dad took me along on a rabbit hunt. At age 4 my enthusiasm for the outdoors was already well established.

CHAPTER II

Early On

IN MANY WAYS, the two men were remarkably similar. Both were children of the Depression and had grown up on hardscrabble hillside farms where they had learned to work hard and long to produce enough food and material things to help their families survive. Both were about six feet tall, about forty years old, lean and hard muscled. They had worked together before, cutting timber with axes and crosscut saws, and dragging logs to the mill with a team of horses. They actually seemed to enjoy physical labor. Each had a young son.

Lewis Carpenter's son was named Paul, and Johnny Vanscoy was my dad. Paul and I were in the same grade in school. Our dads had some interesting ideas about what to do with two boys for entertainment on a Sunday afternoon. We would go groundhog hunting, but not in a conventional way with long range rifles and ammunition; those things were expensive, and money was in short supply. Our dads' choice of weapons was a couple of dogs, shovel, mattock, and a couple of boys for excitement.

Lewis and Paul would show up at our house shortly after noon on Sunday. Lewis had an old hound and our dog was just a mutt. Whichever tool Lewis was carrying, Dad would pick up the other one and away we would go—walking. There were numerous pasture fields very near our small town, and a few minutes of walking would put us in prime "hunting territory." The pasture fields were not level places, knee-deep-in-grass, but hillsides of open areas with interspersed walnut trees, blackberry thickets, and other small brush. It was not ideal pasture for farm animals, but it was an ideal habitat for groundhogs. Landowners didn't mind our intrusions because there was always the possibility of a cow stepping into a hidden hole and breaking a leg.

It was the dogs' job to range ahead and try to catch a groundhog out in the open. A groundhog was always vigilant and almost always won the race to the den opening with a dog right behind him. Once safely inside, he would whistle and snap his teeth in defiance at the frustrated dog outside. The dog's barking would draw the rest of the party to the den entrance and the assault on the besieged groundhog would begin.

Paul and I were assigned the duty of keeping both ourselves and the dogs clear and out of the way. It can be a struggle for a sixty-pound boy to restrain a forty-pound dog with a "let-me-at-him" attitude.

Opening and exposing a sometimes fifty-foot-long groundhog den complex can be a monumental task. Mr. Goundhog is not only an industrious worker but can be a diabolically clever architect as well, taking advantage of tree roots, rock outcroppings, and deceiving twists and turns to provide secure and comfortable accommodations for himself. He also builds at least two or three hidden openings through which he can enter or exit without being noticed.

The main structure of the den will also usually include a kitchen (for eating), a pantry (for food storage), a bedroom (for sleeping or hibernation), and a latrine (for isolating what all animals have to do). There may also be a small alcove or two for loafing, grooming, or just chilling out. As astonishing amounts of dirt, roots, and rocks are extracted from the site, more and more of the den complex is exposed. Finally, a breakthrough is achieved revealing the groundhog or, at least, part of him, and the command is given: "Let 'em go!" The dogs pile into the hole with abandon to snap and grab at that brown fur ball until they get a firm grip. A groundhog is not defenseless

13

and often inflicts some of his own damage with sharp incisors and claws. At this point, a rolling, snapping, snarling ball of two dogs and a groundhog will burst out of the ground, and the groundhog is dispatched by a strong dog bite or a blow from one of the men. This is exciting stuff for a kid! Now the excavation must be backfilled to approximate original contour and we head for home with our trophy. Why? We plan to skin it, cook it, and eat it of course!

* * *

When the time came for berries to ripen, Dad would borrow my grandfather's vehicle and take me to the small farm where he and his five siblings grew up. The farm was situated at the very end of a long hollow and formed a bowl with a couple of level acres of bottomland where the abandoned house and an old barn stood. There was a garden patch behind the house. The remainder of the farm rose 200 to 300 feet vertically, sloping to a ridgeline that nearly encircled the whole farm. A tiny, little brook drained the whole basin, and even in summer, it never dried up. There were blackberries and raspberries growing around the perimeter of the level area, and that was our objective. Dad would pick 3 or 4 gallons while I, with my coffee can, would pick 2 or 3 quarts.

The "bowl" of that farm was a very quiet place and no sounds of human activity intruded. I would listen carefully to the songs of birds that I now know were brown thrashers, cardinals, towhees, wood thrushes, and the occasional red-winged blackbird. From the woods surrounding me I heard phoebes, vireos, yellow warblers, and the hammering of pileated woodpeckers. Sometimes a squirrel would bark and chatter at a real or imagined threat.

I was surprised to find that the little brook was home to a variety of aquatic life. I saw darters, small minnows, frogs, and tadpoles. It seemed that each of the larger stones on the bottom provided shelter for crayfish or hellgrammites. The old barn also provided a couple of surprises. I found some shed snakeskins, and I once startled a barn owl that gave me a full stare before launching from his perch and flying silently away.

After nearly seventy years, I can still remember the old home-place: the fresh air, the green hills, the blue sky, the little brook, and the complete silence. It will always be with me.

* * *

In 1949, I remember the year because I was in first grade, and Doddridge County had its first modern deer season. There weren't many deer back then. They had been pretty much eliminated in our part of the state by the 1920s. In the 1930s, an attempt to reintroduce deer was made in the Arnolds Creek and Bluestone areas by importing about twenty-five deer and releasing them into a large, high-fenced pen where they could be monitored and protected. When World War II came along, the monitoring and fence maintenance failed due to lack of man power.

Trees came down across fences, and the deer began to disperse. By 1949, the deer population had grown enough to declare a short bucks-only season.

The day before the season opened, my grandfather and Dad took me along on a scouting trip in Grandpa's old jeep. We came to an old orchard on a ridge, and Dad took a rail from an old fence and put it up in an apple tree to sit on while he watched for deer the next morning.

The school I attended was on a hill only about 150 yards from our house. Recess came about 10:30, and I eased over to the edge of the playground to check out our house. The jeep was back! I went AWOL, over the hill, and down to our house. Hanging in our garage was the most beautiful animal I had ever seen, and Dad's name was on the tag. It was his first-ever buck.

I floated back up the hill to school and just made it before the bell. I don't think anyone had ever missed me. I was in school the rest of the day, but my mind was chasing deer somewhere in the woods. I have been in love with deer ever since.

In subsequent years, when my uncles and friends came in to deer hunt, they would sit around on a Sunday afternoon, drink coffee, tell stories, and compare rifles and gear. That, for me, was as good as Christmas morning. When I had grown enough to be included, it was even better.

* * *

When my parents paid off the mortgage on our house (yes, people actually did that!), we were able to acquire a car and my horizons were greatly expanded. Some Sundays we would have an early supper and go fishing. (In Appalachia we ate three meals a day. Breakfast was at 6:00 to 6:30 AM, "dinner" was at noon, and "supper" was at 5:30 to 6:00 PM. I once had a smart-mouthed city boy ask me, "Is supper the hillbilly evening meal?" I responded, "Put-down hillbilly jokes are not amusing. We also wear shoes, go to school, and care for our families and neighbors. We work hard. We have respect for God, country, and the rights of others. We are Americans.")

Our fishing destination was usually Middle Island Creek, reputed to be the longest and crookedest "creek" in the world. Its watershed included all or parts of six counties. Its lower reaches were big enough to be named "river" in most places and emptied into the Ohio River. Long and crooked were good descriptions of Middle Island Creek, for in many places the water ran very close to State Route 18. The stream would depart from the road, make a long loop of a mile or two, and return very near the road only a short distance from where it departed. It was a fertile waterway and home to muskies, both largemouth and smallmouth bass, various panfish, catfish, suckers, chubs, freshwater drum, gar, and carp.

Our method of fishing was to park near a loop and wade and fish around the loop and back to the road near the car. We wore old jeans, tennis shoes, T-shirts, and a cap (all washable). We carried rods and reels with which to cast small lures, a pocketful of lures, and a stringer. Fish deemed big enough to keep and eat were trailed along behind us as we waded. Along the way were many indicators of abundant wildlife in the area. Tracks revealed that deer, foxes, raccoons, muskrats, and mink frequently traveled along the stream. The occasional squawk of a little green heron, the rattling of a kingfisher in flight, the harrumph of a bullfrog in the aquatic grass, even the buzzing of cicadas in the trees were constant reminders that this place was full of life.

As twilight approached, we would emerge from the stream and return to the car, carrying our rods and stringers. We usually caught enough fish for a good family meal the next evening.

The walk was always pleasant with fireflies lighting the way and bullfrogs and whip-poor-wills providing music. The rods and fish were stashed away and we headed for home. We were wet and tired but happy and content.

* * *

Middle Island Creek was a very fertile stream with high quality water. Rich in nutrients and soluble minerals, it was an excellent habitat for a wide variety of aquatic life. Freshwater mussels, crayfish, hellgrammites, snails, copepods, and other microscopic organisms were abundant. There were several species of frogs, aquatic insects, and even hellbenders (a giant salamander found only in the Ohio River watershed). A hellbender could be a real nuisance if you were fishing for bass or crappies with live bait because he would grab your bait and retreat under rocks. If you managed to pull him out, he would roll and twist until your hook and three to four feet of your line would be covered with slime. Dealing with that mess was distasteful, but I later learned that hellbenders are one of the best indicators of high-quality water in streams.

We always had a dog, usually a small to medium-sized mixed breed, which was required to possess certain qualifications. He or she had to be very quick, alert, intelligent, and with a strong desire to hunt. Dad would spend some time training the dog to hunt squirrels. It usually didn't take a young dog long to get the hang of treeing squirrels and becoming a team member. He or she was the "finder" and Dad and I were the "shooters." The dog would go ahead of us maintaining about a fifty-yard interval at a slow walking pace. Periodically the dog would stop to silently watch and listen, and we would too. When a squirrel was seen or heard, there was a mad dash to catch it on the ground. That seldom succeeded, as squirrels are very quick to scurry up the nearest tree. Having failed to catch him, the dog would bark up the tree where the squirrel disappeared. Enter the "shooters." We'd go to the tree and take up positions. We carried two guns: a shotgun in case the squirrel ran through the treetops and a scope-sighted .22 rifle. We alternated in "shooter" and "run stopper" positions. At the crack of the .22, the squirrel would tumble out and we were all happy. The dog would grab it and give it a shake, and we would have another squirrel.

If there is a finer meal than fried squirrel, sweet potatoes, gravy, green beans, corn, and hot biscuits, I have never tasted it! My mother would even pack squirrel parts in quart jars, add a little salt and water, and cook them in a pressure cooker. The result was canned squirrel that could be kept for months without refrigeration. (We didn't have a freezer then.) When Mom didn't have time to cook a full meal from scratch, she would open a jar of squirrel, roll the pieces in flour, and brown them in a skillet with butter. The liquid from the jar became gravy. Sweet potatoes, beans, and corn were cooked on the stove, and a full meal would be on the table in about thirty minutes. That was almost as quick as soon-to-be invented TV dinners could be heated, and far better!

* * *

As I grew bigger and older, I was gradually introduced to many other outdoor pursuits. I participated in fox chasing, coon hunting, frog catching, and groundhog hunting with a rifle. I learned to trap mink and muskrats and paid for my own school clothes with my fur profits. Dad taught me to recognize ginseng and yellowroot in the late summer woods, and the sale of those dried roots added to my income.

Almost all my outdoor activities were mentored and monitored by responsible adults. My dad, my grandfather, uncles, neighbors, farmers, and coaches were more than willing to help me learn and grow. These men all believed in being polite, respectful, and law-abiding.

Although many of them were poor and not well educated, they all understood the value of human dignity and hard work, and they would be the first to volunteer whenever someone needed help.

My outdoor experiences made indelible impressions on me as a boy. They were active, exciting times for a seven or eight-year-old, but they later awakened in me a curiosity, interest, even an obsession with the habits, habitats, and behaviors of wild animals. Those experiences would later influence my choice of a career.

CHAPTER III

Transition

WEST VIRGINIA HAS three seasons: fishing season, hunting season, and March! That's not entirely true because there is a time when Mother Nature blesses us with the most glorious season of all: October! The hot doldrums of late summer are replaced by cool, clear skies, crisp mornings with a little frost, beautiful afternoons with no clouds, and sunsets with a tranquility and stillness that calm the soul. An absolute riot of colors emerges from the solid green of the summer, and everywhere you look, you see a calendar picture. The overall impressions you receive are so overwhelming that you'll have trouble recalling them in another month. They defy description. This is the time when nature's efforts reach a crescendo of harvest before the period of rest that is winter. It is magic.

Waterfowl congregate and practice short flights before migration begins. Male deer (bucks) rub their antlers and establish scrapes to begin advertising to does. Groundhogs and bears feed heavily to prepare for hibernation. Squirrels and chipmunks store away provisions for winter. Ruffed grouse experience their "crazy flight" to disperse this year's young to new seasonal ranges. It is a time of preparation driven by hundreds of thousands of years of evolution.

As time passes and the days, seasons, and years go by, change is inevitable. I was growing up and became interested in other things. Football, basketball, baseball, and girls—not necessarily in that order—were occupying much of my time though my passion for the outdoors was undiminished.

In high school, I met a pretty little dark-haired girl who soon became my best friend. We became an "item" and dated through high school and her four years of college. Meanwhile, I was transitioning through several jobs that I did not relish. I worked on construction, for a gas company, in a glass factory, as a shoe salesman, and as a manager of a small warehouse.

In 1964, I was working in the warehouse, and she had taken a job teaching fourth grade. We were married in June. By this time, I realized that if I ever wanted to amount to a "hill of beans," I would need more education. Shelia, my new bride, was very supportive and encouraging. I enrolled in Ohio State University as a part-time student, keeping my day job and attending classes at night. Shelia and I were both working toward a degree: for me a bachelor's and for her a PHT (Putting Hubby Through). At the time, I thought I wanted to be a football coach and teach biology, and I was struggling along through college and university requirements with only a fair grade point average. Working a fifty-hour week and carrying only a few hours of coursework made a degree seem unattainable. Furthermore, I didn't have a lot of interest in art history, music appreciation, or economics 101. Finally, we were able to save enough that Shelia encouraged me to quit my job and become a full-time student. Now a lot more credit hours were possible, and I thought I would soon see the light at the end of the tunnel.

One day, I was taking notes in a class which I was pretty indifferent about and suddenly I had an epiphany. Did I really want to spend the rest of my life in a classroom or on a football field? No! I wanted to be outdoors! I remembered Walt Lesser, a young biologist who had come to our county on his very first job several years before. Walt had told me about some of his work, and as a teenager, I had been fascinated. That night, I went home and searched through the university curriculum catalog and discovered that the botany and zoology department offered coursework leading to a degree in wildlife biology. The next day, I knocked on the door of Dr. Eugene Goode, who would later be my adviser. I asked several questions and quickly decided to change my major. Very soon, I was enjoying coursework in which I was genuinely interested. I was suddenly noticing animals, birds, behaviors, and habitats that had always been there but I had not appreciated due to my own ignorance. Learning was wonderful! My grades began to improve dramatically, and I was on my way. I was eagerly anticipating graduation, finding my outdoor job, and starting a family. However, there was a fly in the ointment. No, it wasn't a fly. It was a big cockroach! Vietnam!

I had previously been called twice by selective service to report for an induction physical. Both times I was classified 1-A. The first time I got a "married" deferment. The second time, I got a full-time student-deferment. When I got the third call, I knew that this time they were going to draft me even though I was a married, full-time student. I couldn't picture myself as a twenty-five-year-old private humping a machine gun through the jungle, so I did the only reasonable thing. I went to the ROTC building, discussed my situation with an army major, and enrolled in Army ROTC. At least the army paid me fifty dollars per month and I could stay in school until I graduated. The night before graduation, Shelia pinned on my lieutenant bars in a commissioning ceremony. The next day, I wore the uniform of a US Army second lieutenant. I received my degree and was officially recognized as an officer, a gentleman, and a graduate of Ohio State University.

Okay. So what's next? I had selected armor as one of my branch choices in the army, hoping that I might get an assignment to Alaska or Germany, so I was not surprised when I was directed to Armor Officers Basic School at Fort Knox, Kentucky. Shelia and I were expecting our first child by then, and we were hoping for a good assignment. Instead, I was assigned to be a training officer in an AIT (Advanced Infantry Training) company at Fort Jackson, South Carolina. All those soldiers were destined for Vietnam. This did not look good.

After a few months, it was about time for us to become parents. I was on a bivouac field training exercise in the middle of the night when the call came that Shelia needed to go to the hospital. I hurried home and drove her to the army hospital where a nurse grabbed Shelia's small suitcase out of my hand and said, "We'll call you at the orderly room." A couple of hours later, I was sitting in the company orderly room drinking coffee and waiting for the hospital to call when a PFC walked in and said, "Are you Lieutenant Vanscoy?" When I said, "Yes," he handed me a thick envelope and said, "Here you go, Sir," and walked out. The envelope contained orders for Vietnam. The call from the hospital about my new daughter came about an hour later. It was a very emotional night.

We traded in our car for a new one to ensure Shelia would have reliable transportation. We bought a mobile home that we set up on my parents' small farm in West Virginia. Shelia got a teaching job in our home county, and both sets of grandparents agreed to help take care of the new baby. Within about three weeks, I had done all I could for my new family. The morning I left, we had about a foot of fresh snow. I hugged and kissed my wife and daughter and set out to an unknown destiny. It was one of the most difficult things I'd ever done. A week or ten days later, I stepped off the plane in Saigon to 100°F heat with 80% humidity.

I won't say much about Vietnam, but I did learn some very valuable life lessons there. Patience, humility, perseverance, and the ability to endure were demonstrated there many times. I've told many people that "I wouldn't take a million dollars for the experience, but I wouldn't do it again for two million." While I was in the field, I made it into Saigon, placed my rifle in a corner, sat for the Graduate Record Exam, picked up my rifle, and returned to the field. I must have done pretty well because I was accepted for graduate work at all three of the universities to which I applied. At the end of my one-year tour of duty, I had not been wounded, I had not had to kill anyone, and I was more than ready to come home. When I returned to a loving family, a safe and secure home, and no pressing obligations, I felt like the richest man in the world.

CHAPTER IV

A Real Job

AT THIS POINT, there was nothing I had to do right away, so I spent the next couple of months convincing my little daughter that "Daddy" was a real person and not just a voice from the tape recorder. Lori, my seventeen-month-old daughter, and I would play and go for walks once my own mother decided that I was indeed a responsible adult capable of caring for my own child. I spent time with family and friends, relaxed, went to a few dinners, and even spoke at a couple of VFW (Veterans of Foreign Wars) meetings. It was wonderful. As the end of Shelia's school year approached, I began to feel the itch to move on, so I took a temporary job as a summer youth program coordinator. I had planned to return to school in the fall to complete the requirements for a master's degree. One day, I happened to be in Charleston, so I dropped into the wildlife division office to introduce myself and to inquire about future job prospects.

I left without a lot of encouragement about future employment. A few days later, I received a call at home describing a new position they were starting and asking if I would be interested. The job description was perfect, but the salary was less than I would receive from GI Bill and a fellowship, and I had a family to support. I explained all that, thanked them for the call and the offer, and indicated that I would be returning to school. To my surprise, I got another call about a week later saying they had decided to increase the salary for that position and wondered if I would be interested at $——— a year? I don't remember the exact amount. (It would seem pitifully small today.) I requested a day or two to discuss it with my wife. I immediately placed calls to the three professors I knew who were heads of wildlife research units at their respective universities. When they heard the particulars, all three advised me to take the job. They even said that they had masters graduates who couldn't find wildlife jobs. That made the decision pretty easy. I took the job.

The job description called for taking an office in one of the ranger districts on the Monongahela National Forest. The Forest Service would provide office space, clerical help, and logistical support in the form of topographic maps, road and trail maps, and keys to any areas restricted from the public. The work was to examine any proposed timber sales or forest compartment designations, assess the value of particular sections of forest to wildlife, and write recommendations to the Forest Service to mitigate or enhance the impact of a logging operation on the local wildlife. Duties also included working with the resident wildlife managers (state DNR employees) to assist them in their efforts to improve or maintain wildlife habitat and to assist in wildlife research projects emanating from our Elkins Operations Center.

There were three positions I could choose from, so Shelia and I packed a picnic, lots of baby stuff, and a map and set out on a long day's drive to visit these small towns and figure out where we would most like to live. Our parents followed in a second car to enjoy the drive, to see where we would be living, and to help with the baby and picnic. I think they were secretly relieved that their tenure as part-time babysitters would soon end. We were a happy group.

* * *

For a number of reasons, we chose to move to Richwood. It was home of the Gauley Ranger District, which included the Cranberry Backcountry, a 50,000-plus-acre wilderness, and many thousand other acres of National Forest, including several campgrounds, picnic areas, hiking trails, and three of the best trout streams in the state: the Williams, the Cranberry, and the Cherry Rivers. I could hardly wait to start to work.

We discovered that Richwood had a shortage of good housing, but we found a small trailer park that had an open slot. We moved into town bringing our home with us. In three or four days, we were all set up with a small yard and a little shed for a lawn mower and some other odds and ends. A couple of days at the Elkins Operations Center for introductions, orientation, review of work rules, issue of uniforms and equipment and I was ready to get started.

Somehow in only five months, I had come from a tropical combat zone halfway around the world to the cool mountains of my home state to a "Ranger Rick" job with a four-wheel-drive truck doing biological stuff in a friendly forest. It would become a thirty-two-year adventure.

On my first day in my new office, I was sitting at my desk nursing a cup of coffee and studying some maps when I sensed a person standing in the open door. I looked up and saw a stocky middle-aged man wearing a DNR uniform. He had the look of someone who was accustomed to hard work. He wore a bemused smile, and his name tag said Paul Hill, wildlife manager.

"You must be Mr. Vanscoy," he said.

I said, "No, Sir. I'm Bill. Mr. Vanscoy is my dad. He lives up in Doddridge County."

As it turned out, that was a good response. Paul's smile changed to a grin. He came in and shook my hand, and we began to get to know each other over coffee. I soon learned that Paul had grown up in Southern West Virginia, served in the Pacific Theater of World War II, returned home to work in the coal mines for a time, and then became a wildlife manager for the WVDNR (West Virginia Division of Natural Resources). He was indeed accustomed to hard work, and he knew how to do a lot of things.

When there was a job to be done, he did not tarry nor did he hurry. He would consider the work and get it finished with an economy of motion at a steady pace that was exemplary. Paul was very conscientious about his work, and he took excellent care of his equipment. He also had a quick dry wit that would sometimes crack me up.

One day, we were working together in the Cranberry Backcountry and stopped to eat our bag lunches. I needed to drain off some coffee, so I stepped away from the truck. As I was getting relief, I was looking around and spotted a huge four-prong ginseng that was about three feet tall. I finished, took out my pocket knife, and snipped off the top of the plant, got back in the truck, and laid it up on the dash. Paul studied it while he chewed and swallowed a bite of sandwich. He said, "Wow, that's a really big one!" I unwrapped my own sandwich and said, "I'd like to have a good ginseng dog (there's no such thing of course). I might take up ginsenging again."

Paul said, "I had one once. He was a good one, too, but the kids ruined him."

I said, "Really? How so?"

In a sad voice, he said, "They got him to barking at mayapple."

When I met one of Paul's children for the first time, a very attractive young lady, I couldn't resist teasing him a little bit.

I said, "Paul, as homely as you are, how can you have such a good-looking daughter?"

He immediately replied, "I was thinking beautiful thoughts when she was conceived!"

On many occasions, while driving through the forest, we would encounter blowdowns that were blocking the road or trail. Paul would calmly retrieve his chain saw from his toolbox, clear the tree in twenty-inch chunks from the road, brush off and store the chain saw, load up the chunks of log, and we would be on our way in ten to fifteen minutes. Those chunks would be unloaded at the wildlife management shop/storage building where there was a woodstove to help warm the building. Later, Paul would stand a two-to-three-foot diameter chunk on end and walk around it, calmly knocking off stove bolt-sized pieces with each swing of his ax. He made it look easy. I tried it. It wasn't!

CHAPTER V

New Things

IN THE NEXT several months, there were a bunch of firsts that I had not anticipated. One was my first encounter with a wild black bear. I was exploring a section of the Cranberry Backcountry and was following an old, overgrown log road to see if it joined with another, better used road in the next drainage. The road became so narrow that I knew there was not going to be enough room to turn around. I certainly didn't want to get stuck there, miles from anyone. I stopped the truck and decided to walk the road ahead to see if I could drive through or find a place to turn around. I picked up a small stick with which I could knock down spiderwebs that were stretched across my path.

I had walked about a quarter of a mile when I rounded a small bend in the road and spotted a movement in the foliage about fifty yards ahead. A little more movement by something black and some scratching sounds convinced me that this was a flock of wild turkeys. I had almost no experience with turkeys, and I wanted to observe them, so I went into sneak mode to try to get closer. I had about cut the distance in half when I heard a loud *whoof* and a crash and a bear came bounding up the trail at me. In about a nanosecond, I realized that I couldn't outrun or outclimb a bear, and I certainly couldn't defend myself with a small stick, so I did the only thing that occurred to me. I threw my hands into the air to appear as large as possible and shouted at the top of my lungs, "Hey, Bear!" The bear skidded to a stop about thirty feet away and stood up on its back legs to get a better look at me. This made me feel a little better, so I shouted again, "Why don't you get your butt out of here?" It did! It whirled and bolted back the way it had come. In seconds, it disappeared back into the foliage and was gone without a sound. I just stood there, limp with relief for a few moments, and thought about what had just happened. If the bear was a boar, it would be most likely afraid of me and long gone. If the bear was a sow with cubs, she might still be nearby and willing to do battle for their sake. I decided to take the advice I had shouted at the bear, and I was not slow in walking back to my truck.

A black bear can be pretty imposing when
you meet one up close in the forest.
Photo by Steven Rotsch

* * *

The DNR at that time had an ongoing wild turkey restoration program. The idea was to livetrap turkeys from areas where they were numerous and transport and release them as quickly as possible in areas that had no turkeys but had once again become good turkey habitat. Although neither of us had turkey-trapping experience, Paul and I were assigned to catch birds on the Gauley District. We were familiar with the equipment (I had used a cannon net in college), and we were coached and given tips by some of the biologists. It is easier to entice birds to bait sites when food is scarce, so we were trapping in the winter. We had a four-wheel-drive truck with snow tires, chains on all four wheels, a winch on the front, and a truck bed full of log chunks. On several occasions, I had to pull out that winch line through waist-deep snow to get us through snowdrifts. Turkey trapping also took a terrible toll on glass thermos bottles. I can still remember the liquid *scrunch* when one hit the floor of the pickup. Luckily, Santa brought me a stainless steel-vacuum bottle for Christmas.

We'd been informed that they now needed only hen turkeys to complete the program, so we kept going. Finally, we had a good flock on bait, everything was ready, and we were in our pop-up blind well before daylight. Paul was watching through a small port, and shortly after good light, he nudged me and whispered, "They're here."

I whispered back and said, "Wait till their heads are all down."

I glanced out my peephole and saw about twenty birds on the site and looked down to get ready to fire the net. Shortly, Paul said, "Shoot." I touched the wires to the terminals and boom! We bolted out of the blind and quickly secured our catch. We had nine birds, but they were all gobblers. We banded them and released them at the site. It was our first catch! We could do this! We later contributed hens to a program that was very successful at restoring turkeys throughout the state.

* * *

Throughout West Virginia at higher elevations (generally above 1,500–2,000 feet), there is a specific plant that is one of the first to emerge and grow as the snow recedes in the spring. It is a first cousin of onions, shallots, and may be related to garlic. It grows from roots in clusters and forms slender bulbs with two main leaves that resemble spinach or a flattened onion leaf. It has been consumed by Native Americans for hundreds of years and has recently been embraced by gourmet chefs and high-end restaurants as a soup, garnish, salad, or flavor-enhancer for exotic dishes. The entire plant, sans roots, is edible and is in high demand in many big cities, where it can be expensive. It is called the ramp or, if you like snob appeal, the "ramson." Though it can be cultivated, it also commonly grows in thick beds in the woods. There are two types: one grows through a purplish sheath and is considered to be stronger and more pungent, and the other grows through a white sheath and is considered to be more delicate in flavor. Gathering ramps is a common pursuit in springtime Appalachia. Poems and songs are written, festivals are organized, parades are held, churches and civic groups put on ramp dinners, and even beauty pageants celebrate to recognize the mighty ramp. The only problem is that eating ramps will make your breath—and for some, your whole body—stink. If people around you have eaten ramps, you must also eat some in self-defense. That way, the smell won't bother you.

There was a well-known man in Richwood named Jim Comstock who owned a newspaper called the *West Virginia Hillbilly*. Mr. Comstock was the owner, publisher, editor, reporter, typesetter, commentator, and distributor of the paper. He was never shy about offering an opinion on any subject whether or not it was controversial. One spring, he mixed the juice of crushed ramps with printer's ink, published the edition, and mailed copies to subscribers all over the country. He was reprimanded by the US Postal Service who threatened to deny him their service. He took pride in the fact that his was the only newspaper in the country that was censored by the federal government.

Paul and I had stopped for lunch, and I was getting out a sandwich when Paul said, "Bill, have you ever eaten ramps?"

I said, "No. They don't grow in my home county."

He said, "There's a big patch right here by the truck, and they're white ones too!"

I got out and gathered a few, snipped off the roots and leaves, and covered my roast beef sandwich with them as you might do with onion slices. I thought they were quite good. That night after dinner and a shower, Shelia and I were ready for bed and she said, "You stink so bad I can't stand you." She went to bed in another bedroom. That was the first and last time I ever put raw ramps on a sandwich.

* * *

Although I had been introduced to many aspects of wildlife biology in college, I still did not truly appreciate the subtleties and complexities of the scientific method as it applies to wildlife management.

That was about to change. Dr. Frank Hayes, along with a team of scientists and graduate students from the Southeastern Cooperative Wildlife Disease Study (SCWDS) at the University of Georgia, came to West Virginia to help the WVDNR better understand our ruffed grouse population. These people brought a level of expertise that we could not duplicate. We DNR were to collect a sample of grouse from each of the main categories of forest types in the state, including northern hardwoods, oak-hickory, and mixed bottomland. Paul and I were assigned to collect birds from northern hardwoods. It took us three long days to collect our quota. The real eye-opener though came when we watched the SCWDS take those birds apart in minute detail. In addition to a thorough examination for any and all parasites—both external and internal—the birds were aged, sexed, weighed, measured, and all data was carefully recorded. Any evidence of current or past disease was collected and analyzed microscopically. All of this information yields a good picture of the current health of the grouse population, but when compared with data from past or future collections, it can reveal trends that are valuable in making good wildlife management decisions. The same principles apply to all species. The more you know about a given species, the more efficiently you can manipulate the habitat to enhance the survival and well-being of that species. This is a simple concept, but a lot of hard work, funding, perseverance, and insight are required to achieve success. For the first time, I began to realize what the science of wildlife biology was all about.

In their wisdom, our founding fathers decided that fish and game (indeed all wildlife) should belong to all the people and not to a few elite or royalty. This was critically important to early settlers, as most of them depended on wildlife for food. As the years went by, various laws were enacted to conserve wildlife and to ensure that the benefits of that wildlife were equally available to all the people. Later on, licenses, fees, and taxes were instituted to provide funding for law enforcement, research, and habitat management. In other words, hunters and fishermen—people who loved wildlife and enjoyed its benefits—were paying the bill to conserve it. Conservation, by the way, is defined as "protecting from loss, damage, or injury." Something being "conserved" can be used and enjoyed as long as loss, damage, or injury does not occur. This concept became known around the world as the North American Conservation Model and is envied by many other countries. Most of the people in the world do not have access to wildlife or the freedom to enjoy what we sometimes take for granted.

CHAPTER VI

Understanding

LONG BEFORE I ever started to school, I fully understood that if the preacher and his wife were coming for dinner, somebody had to kill a chicken. Food did not just magically appear on the table. Somebody had to kill something for meat. Somebody had to plant, cultivate, and harvest plants for salads and vegetables. Somebody had to squeeze a teat for milk, butter, and cheese. Somebody had to refine, process, and cook all these raw ingredients to produce a meal on the table. Though all this work is not always pleasant, it is necessary if we want to eat. This has been true since the dawn of time. Everything eats because something has lived before it.

There are those who would argue that microbes on the ocean floor can synthesize food from minerals oozing from fissures in the earth's crust, but who's to say that these minerals were not once part of a life cycle a very long time ago? Mother Nature wastes nothing and recycles everything. Life and death are normal and natural events that occur every day.

There's a term commonly used in wildlife biology that must be understood if we're attempting to manage any living thing. That term is population dynamics. What it means is this: a population of any species (we'll use white-tailed deer for example) is never stable. It is always increasing or decreasing. In a year's time, it will go from a low to a high to a low population again. The low point for deer is usually in March and April when hunter harvest, harsh winter weather, disease, starvation, accidents, and predation have reduced the population. In May and June, when fawns are born, the population spikes to a high point, and the cycle begins again. The amazing thing about deer is that if you have 100,000 and there are no catastrophes, you will have 100,000 at the same time next year even if 40,000 die during the year. This example is oversimplified, but the basic premise is true and is vital in wildlife management.

It follows then that the life or death of a single individual is of very little significance to the overall population. This brings into play the disciplines of probability and statistics, but management is not about number crunching alone. Many other factors such as weather, disease, predation, harvest, habitat change, financing, public opinion, etc. must be considered. Wildlife management is a little bit like a juggler trying to keep several balls in the air at the same time.

Another term that is commonly used in wildlife management is carrying capacity. This is a concept that is generally imperfectly understood to mean the numbers of a given species that can be sustained by a finite area of habitat. This definition assumes that the quality of habitat will remain the same, but this is not the case. Habitat is also dynamic and may be altered by fire, flooding, storms, natural succession, or the activities of man. Habitat that is ideal for one species may be an absolute desert for another species. For example, pileated woodpeckers cannot survive in marshland, and red-winged blackbirds can't survive in a solid canopy mature forest. Each type of habitat has characteristics which will affect the success of all species living there. These are known as limiting factors, which includes availability of food, shelter from weather, sometimes disease and parasites, predators, and suitable areas for producing and rearing young.

When conditions are favorable for a given species, those animals soon fill up the habitat to a point where one or more limiting factors will kick in and stabilize the numbers of that species. That stabilized number is said to be the carrying capacity.

A good example of carrying capacity would be the ruffed grouse. Around 1950 in West Virginia, thousands of acres in the north central part of the state were beginning the natural succession of old farms back into young forest. This regrowth was a boon for ruffed grouse as their ideal habitat is edge which provides abundant food, cover, and protection for broods of chicks. The primo years for natural succession to produce ideal grouse cover are about fifteen to thirty, so the best (and most) habitat occurred from the mid-60s to the mid-90s. I became a serious grouse hunter in the early 1970s and for several years enjoyed a grouse population that would often yield twenty plus flushes in a half day. By the mid-1980s, it was obvious that the grouse population in North Central West Virginia was shrinking. There were three main reasons for the grouse decline: (1) Natural succession was causing the cover to grow out, (2) a rapid expansion of the deer herd resulted in browsing that further reduced the understory cover, and (3) the reintroduction of wild turkeys and their success created competition for food. The habitat that had been ideal for grouse had changed and now the carrying capacity for grouse had become much less.

When the numbers of animals of a given species exceed the carrying capacity of the habitat for that species, the population will inevitably crash. This sudden decline will be due to starvation or a host of other factors, but it will happen. Unfortunately, a population crash usually results in changes to the original habitat that will reduce the carrying capacity. The postcrash habitat will now support fewer animals than it once did.

I sometimes wonder what the Earth's carrying capacity for humanity might be!

Earlier, I mentioned the inevitability of change. The demographic of the American people has changed so much in the last fifty years that I now hardly recognize us. The bulk of our population has shifted from rural to urban or suburban so radically that many common skills have disappeared. Many of us no longer even know the basics of how to feed ourselves. We suppose that milk comes from a plastic jug, meat is on a Styrofoam platter, chicken tenders and fish fillets come in a frozen plastic bag, vegetables come in little frozen boxes, drinks are obtained from bottles on the shelf, and even our morning coffee comes from Starbucks. I would bet that there are plenty of coffee drinkers who have no idea how to brew their own.

This drastic population shift has some far-reaching ramifications. Small family farms are not only not profitable, many have become uninhabitable because they are so far removed from the places where we earn our living. Technology and mechanization have taken over food production, and only large corporate farms can turn a profit. Families, too, have undergone drastic changes. Dad now works in an office. Mom probably has a job in addition to driving the kids to soccer practice, little league, music lessons, etc. The kids attend school, various summer camps, and numerous organized sports activities. We just don't have time anymore to appreciate or even notice the natural world around us.

Not long ago, I backed my pickup truck out of a space in the Walmart parking lot and started up the lane toward the exit. I saw four people walking toward me and the store entrance. They were walking abreast and each was looking at a device in his or her hands. They looked like Mom, Dad, and two adolescent kids, a girl and a boy. None of them looked up, so I stopped and waited. Finally, at about three paces, the man and the two kids glanced up, saw me, and veered to the side. The woman never glanced up, walked into the center of my grill, almost dropped her phone, stepped around my truck, and kept walking without ever taking her eyes off her phone. What kind of people can be that oblivious to their surroundings? If they were subject to "survival of the fittest," they'd be goners for sure. On the other hand, we now have a whole generation with the quickest thumbs in the history of mankind!

* * *

Since humans have been walking upright and living together in groups, there have always been a few individuals who possess exceptional abilities. They may or may not have been the biggest, fastest, or strongest in their group, but they had other skills and abilities which enabled them to survive better than their peers. Their eyesight, sense of smell, hearing, reflexes, memory, ability to discern relationships and improve through experience made them better hunters and gatherers. They were icons in their society.

As agriculture enabled people to stop wandering and settle in one place, our focus began to change. We no longer had to worry about our next meal, so we shifted our adulation to people who exhibited exceptional physical abilities. We have invented a myriad of competitions to measure physical abilities, and the winners became icons.

To my knowledge, there are no competitions that measure survivability in the natural world. The unique combination of abilities and skills that make us one with nature is difficult to define and almost impossible to measure, but to ignore the importance of nature would be a big mistake.

There are many of us who still value outdoor skills even though those skills may no longer be necessary to ensure our survival. We can always get what we need at the grocery store. People have asked me, "Why do you hunt and fish if it is no longer necessary?" Many outdoorsmen have heard the same question and struggled to give a satisfactory answer because the real answers are elusive and hard to articulate. I will attempt an answer.

I hunt and fish because I am fascinated by spiderwebs glistening with dew before the sun comes up; because I love the gurgling sounds of a rushing stream; because fall colors fill me with wonder; because geese honk, turkeys gobble, and elk bugle; because bait skips and flees on the surface when fish are feeding; because sunrise signals a new day and sunset says it is time to rest. I hunt and fish because woodpeckers, jays, and chickadees enliven a silent winter woodland; because I can see, hear, and smell the amazing productivity of a salt marsh; because the strain of climbing a hill or wading through swift water brings satisfaction that I can do it. I hunt and fish because the warmth of sunshine, the discomfort of rain, the chill of frost and snow always remind me that I am subject to all the changes of weather that every living thing must endure or enjoy. I hunt and fish because I am a part of it. I am a predator and a participant in life or death. If I went afield as a painter or photographer, I would only be an observer or recorder. As a participant, I am an integral part of life cycles, I can enjoy and appreciate the results, I can retain my sanity and rest securely in the knowledge that all living things are subject to the laws of nature. I can savor the excitement and anticipation of preparing for an outing, enjoy each moment afield, and be fulfilled at the end of the day. I do not need to hunt and fish in order to have food, but I do need to hunt and fish in order to be a complete person. Thousands of years of surviving with nature have engraved on my DNA the need to be a full-fledged participant in the cycle of life.

CHAPTER VII

People

THE PEOPLE I met, worked with, and interacted with in Richwood were friendly, helpful, and courteous. The entire Forest Service staff from the district ranger to the most recently hired temporary laborer were all quick to help, answer questions, or give much-needed advice. The people of Richwood were much the same, whether it was in the bank, the grocery store, the hardware store, or the auto repair shop. The people at church were welcoming, and Shelia and I soon had many friends and lots of acquaintances. The DNR folks I worked with were much like Army brothers-in-arms because success for any one of us was seen as a success for all of us. It was a very good situation in which to live and work.

There were a few incidents and brief interactions that I will always remember. It was not unusual for the crew at the local fish hatchery to be shorthanded when trout stocking day rolled around, and, in a pinch, they would call Paul or me to request help. If we had nothing important scheduled, we'd meet the stock truck and spend a few hours distributing trout in the local streams. We were stocking fish in the Cranberry River, and there was a particular pool which was long and very deep where we usually put four or five dip nets of fish. This was in the Cranberry Backcountry behind locked gates where public access was restricted to foot or bicycle travel only. A very large rock hung over the pool where we could stand and drop fish into the water, and I had just dropped the first net and was turning around when I was pushed from behind by an elderly fisherman who had appeared suddenly out of nowhere. In his haste to get his hook and line in the water, he had very nearly knocked me off the rock and into the pool. I returned to the truck steaming. Paul was up on the truck dipping and handing down nets of fish. I just stood there for a moment. Paul looked at me, shook his head, and said, "Don't do it." I threw the net up on top of the truck and said, "Let's go."

By the time we reached our next stop, I had cooled off. Paul looked over at me with a smile and said, "You were going to knock him off there, weren't you?"

I smiled and said, "Yeah, but the old goat probably couldn't swim, and I'd have had to pull him out."

We both had a good laugh, and the extra trout were stocked elsewhere.

* * *

The town of Richwood is surrounded by mountains that prob-ably reach 3,000 to 3,500 feet in elevation. At or near the ridgelines, there is a very good air drainage which allows orchards to flourish. There was one old farmstead that had a cabin, an outbuilding, and a small orchard of two or three dozen apple trees. The owner lived in Richwood and only visited the farm occasionally. One evening, he called me and went into a rant about how the bears were destroying his orchard. Though I doubted that he had ever made a penny from selling apples, I reassured him that we would check it out and, if need be, trap and remove the culprits. The next morning, Paul and I went to assess the situation. Now it must be understood that bears are not the most delicate of foragers. Their method of apple picking is to climb a tree and eat everything they can reach. When whatever limb they are on becomes shaky and threatens to break, they simply reach out and break the limb back toward them to get the apples growing near the end. There was a good bit of damage, and even some claw and tooth marks on the cabin and outbuilding. Now we had to do something.

The only culvert trap that was readily available was not on a trailer. A culvert trap is a ten-foot section of four-foot culvert with a heavy grid welded over one end and a heavy solid guillotine door and frame over the other. The trigger is near the grid and releases the door at the other end, thereby trapping the bear. These culvert traps are usually mounted on a low trailer for ease of transport, but the one we had was without wheels and had to be manhandled. We managed to load the trap, haul it to the farm, get it off-loaded, baited, and set. This all took place on Friday.

Early on Saturday morning, Shelia and I decided to make the two-and-a-half-hour drive to visit our parents. We were expecting our second child and thought it would be best to visit before riding in the car became too uncomfortable for her. Besides, our daughter wanted to see her grandparents. It turned out to be a short visit.

On Sunday, about 6:30 AM, the phone rang. It was Paul. He had gone early to check the trap, and we had a bear. I asked him to call the bear biologist in Elkins, hurriedly packed up, and headed home. By the time I got back to the trap site about 10:00 AM, the biologist from Elkins had arrived, along with what looked like half the population of Richwood. From the sign Paul and I had observed, we had expected to catch a sow with one or two cubs, but this bear was a very large boar, and he was not happy to be in that trap. When the bear biologist saw what we had, he immediately proclaimed, "We might as well turn him loose right here because he'll be back in two or three days no matter where we release him."

I quickly grabbed his elbow and steered him aside and said, "We promised the landowner that we'd remove the bear, and that's just what we're going to do!"

There were enough men standing around to help lift trap, bear, and all into the bed of a pickup, and we drove away with the bear throwing such a fit that the truck was rocking from side to side. We released him nearly fifty miles away, and as far as I know, he never came back.

* * *

As autumn was approaching, the anticipation of hunting season was growing in Richwood. Many of the local residents were hunters or related to hunters, and casual conversations often turned to discussions about deer, bears, turkeys, grouse, or rabbits. Considerable attention was given to the weather and specific locations for hunting deer. Comparisons of the relative merits of calibers, action types, and sights for deer rifles were frequently heard all over town. Boots, clothing, and knives were popular subjects in a community where opening day was the equivalent of a national holiday. Everyone was getting ready.

Given this atmosphere, I was not surprised to receive a call from Jim Comstock of the *West Virginia Hillbilly*. He wanted to ask some questions about the upcoming deer season, and I agreed to stop by his office that afternoon for an interview. During the course of a friendly forty-five-minute conversation, I made the comment that a healthy adult doe on good range would normally produce two fawns each year. That week, when the *Hillbilly* came out, I was quoted as saying a healthy adult doe on good range would normally produce fawns twice each year. I was surprised and chagrined, so I quickly called Mr. Comstock and explained the error. I also said, "People who know about deer will think one of two things: either I'm stupid or you are! I don't care about myself, but I wouldn't want them to think that about you, so in the future, please allow me to review a quote before you print it."

He laughed, apologized, and agreed. He said, "I can take the heat. I've been wrong before."

In the course of less than two months, I had learned three valuable lessons about dealing with people. First, in the case of the fisherman, never act on impulse, but pause to consider the possible repercussions of your actions. Second, in the case of the landowner, always be honest, and do what you say you're going to do. Third, in the case of the editor, always be certain others understand exactly what you're telling them, and be as diplomatic as possible in the telling.

CHAPTER VIII

Working on Gauley

As SHELIA AND I were expecting our second child, another deer season was approaching and wildlife biologists and managers were called to a preseason meeting at Handley Public Hunting Area about fifty miles away. Shelia assured me that she'd be fine, as she had a doctor's appointment that afternoon and that the baby wasn't due for another week. About midafternoon, the phone at Handley rang. It was Shelia. She had gone to the doctor's office, and upon a quick examination, he told her to go straight to the hospital to deliver. Instead, she drove home, found a babysitter, called me, grabbed her little suitcase, and drove herself to the hospital. I arrived about an hour and fifteen minutes later and found her sitting comfortably in a bed with a big smile on her face. She said, "It's going to be awhile, and another woman is in delivery, so why don't you go down to the cafeteria and get a bite to eat. We still have plenty of time."

I hurried downstairs, inhaled a hamburger and a soda, and hustled back to her room. She had already gone to delivery, and they wouldn't let me go in. In less than an hour, I was informed that we had another daughter and everyone was just fine. I did not get to see either of my daughters being born. The addition of another person to our small family made us aware that we would need more room, both in our housing and in our car. We soon were considering a bigger car and more spacious housing.

Meanwhile, deer season was upon us, and I was sure to be busy. The buildup to opening day was becoming obvious everywhere. Campers were arriving and getting set up all over the National Forest. Towable trailers were arriving at campgrounds, and backpackers were entering the Cranberry Backcountry. There were several serious deer camps that were traditional, and the methods of getting into the backcountry were often ingenious and well planned. One family—father, sons, sons-in-law, and grandsons—had camped for several years in the same clearing where Dogway Run emptied into the Cranberry River. Their method of arrival was to take turns pushing a homemade tricycle/trailer down the Dogway Run Road to the Cranberry. Their camp consisted of a large wall tent, wood-burning stove, a table, chairs, and sleeping bags—everything they needed for a week in the wilderness. At the end of the week, they would load everything back in their "vehicle" and push it down the Cranberry River Road to the locked gate at the Cranberry campground. (No private motor vehicles were allowed in the backcountry area.) The roadways were mostly descending and they were cheerful in their work though the total distance was about twenty-five miles. Others would use horses or mules, and some would backpack and sleep in pup tents. These folks were serious about their deer hunting.

Paul and I were assigned to patrol the backcountry, check on the camps to ensure that everyone was okay, check and tag the deer harvested, and take successful hunters and their deer to the locked gates if they wished. All their other stuff was their responsibility. This was a fun job, as we enjoyed meeting the hunters, collecting data on deer, and hearing about the adventures of hunters. The only problem was the weather. The temperature fell to around 0°F and we had about 1 to 1½ feet of snow.

There were two incidents with animals which I will always remember. First, I was coming through the backcountry on Friday before the Monday opener, and I decided to stop at the mouth of Dogway Run to see if the family camp had arrived. I got out of my truck and walked up toward the clearing which had some apple trees scattered around. When I saw the clearing was empty, I turned back toward the truck and I noticed something dark moving in one of the apple trees. My first thought was that perhaps some archery hunter had left something in the tree and the wind was causing it to move. As I got closer, I realized that it was a bear trying to get the last few apples. I suppose the wind shifted because the bear suddenly froze in mid-reach, looked in my direction, and, in a panic, tried to turn around on a small limb. He failed and fell. He tried one last paw grab at the limb which caused him to cartwheel to the ground where he landed with a *whomph* on his back. In an instant, he was galloping for the nearest woods where he stopped and stared in my direction as if to say, "What the h—— was that?" I laughed all the way back to the truck.

The second incident was on Saturday at the end of the first week of deer season. Cold and snow had become too much for another camp and they were pulling out. They had a mule and a small buckboard, but they were heading uphill back to the locked gate at the head of Dogway Run. They had taken three deer which were on top of the camping gear in the buckboard. When we came up to them, five men were carrying all they could while trying to help push or pull the buckboard through eighteen inches of snow. The mule was staggering and limping badly. They all looked to be in bad shape. We stopped, checked and tagged the deer, put the hunters and their deer and some of their gear on our truck, and drove the five miles or so up to the gate where we unloaded, turned around, and started back down Dogway Run Road. Around the first bend, we met the mule which was now trotting along like a sulky pacer. The relief of most of the buckboard load and the knowledge that he was going home had caused that mule to make a most miraculous recovery!

* * *

As winter loosened its grip on the mountains, I was out one day walking over and evaluating a proposed timber sale on the lower part of the district. I came across a fallen log that aroused my curiosity. It was about forty-feet long, covered with moss, and the top limbs and root ball had rotted away (not surprising in an environment where 60% of the days have some form of precipitation). Standing at the middle of the log, I could not see over it. Though I'm only 5'8", that is still a very large log, and all the bark and some of the exterior wood was gone also. I used my knife to cut down to solid wood and discovered that it was American chestnut. I stood there for a while, thinking about the tree it must have been. It was probably a sprout or seedling about 1700 when Cherokee and Seneca used this area as a hunting ground. By the middle of the century, it was a firm young tree just establishing its place in the canopy. It had witnessed small family groups of bison, elk, deer, black bear, mountain lions, timber wolves, wild turkeys, and of course squirrels. It had also hosted hordes of passenger pigeons. By the time of George Washington's surveying exploits and through the French and Indian War and the American Revolution, it had become a dominant tree in the canopy. It survived the War of 1812 and even the Civil War only to die in the 1920s from chestnut blight and fall in a storm a few years later. How I wished that tree could have told me its whole story! I'm sure that if we could review the changes that occurred in the Appalachians during the life of that tree, we would be more attuned to our environment and more careful about how we use our natural resources.

In a small town like Richwood, the nearby presence of many thousands of acres of National Forest affected just about everyone. Of course, there were Forest Service employees, but there were also many other occupations that were involved with activities in the forest. Timber cutters, bulldozer operators, road builders, cabinet and furniture makers, auto sales and repair shops, grocery and hardware stores, hydroseeding and reclamation outfits, truckers, outdoor shops, and naturally lots of hunters and fishermen were all very interested in the current and future management of the forest. All of these people had opinions on what should or should not be done, and no two opinions are exactly alike. Some said that cutting timber was fine, while some wanted no cutting at all. Some said clear-cutting was good, while others argued that selective cutting was preferable. Some said the cuts were too big, while others said they were too small. Some said cuts were too close to roads or streams, while others thought buffer zones were adequate. And on and on went the controversies.

The Forest Service does indeed have a long-range master plan that is a model for eastern hardwood forest management. At some point, future generations will enjoy a diversified forest that provides for recreation, timber, wildlife, and watershed control, but it will require time and resources to achieve that goal. It will not be a quick fix. While wildlife management can frequently show results in two or three years, the results of forest management usually require decades. In modern society, our demands for instant gratification have ruined our appreciation of the virtues of patience, humility, perseverance, and endurance. We are poorer for the loss.

As I spent more time in the woods on the Gauley Ranger District, I met many people who were avid outdoorsmen, and a lot of them had some interesting questions. Should I be afraid of bears? Why can't I see trout in the water where I can see every rock on the bottom? Are there fewer deer here than there are in Ritchie County? Can a bobcat kill a deer? What tore up all the leaves on the ground just up this trail? Why don't I see lots of squirrels in all these woods? As I tried my best to answer these and many other questions, I began to realize that these people were certainly not dumb. They were just sorely in need of information and exposure to nature. In my mind, the need for public education about wildlife management and habitat manipulation was coming into focus.

CHAPTER IX

A New Job

As SPRING PROGRESSED, an unfortunate accident took the life of one of our DNR employees. This man had been superintendent of French Creek Game Farm, a well-known DNR facility. After a respectful period of time, the open position was announced and applications were being accepted.

Shelia and I discussed this new possibility at length. Although I loved the job I had, I could not envision that it would have a long-term impact on the wildlife in West Virginia, and I wanted to do something that would make a difference. At French Creek, I would be able to meet lots of people and perhaps influence them in favor of wildlife. Besides, it was closer to our families, it came with a residence provided, and it would be a great place for our kids to grow up and go to school. We made the drive to French Creek to check it out, liked what we saw, and I submitted my application. A few weeks later, I was told that I had a new job.

Executing the move would be problematic. We had two small children, we needed to sell our mobile home, the residence needed some work, and I needed to take over the operation and maintenance of the game farm. Our solution was for Shelia and the kids to stay in Richwood while I got things at French Creek ready for our move.

I would work in the office or on the area until quitting time, work in the residence until the wee hours, and then sleep until it was time for work the next day. There was painting, repairing plaster, laying carpet, and refurbishing the kitchen. I would return to Richwood on weekends and help with packing up. Finally, after about three or four weeks, we were ready to move. We had sold our mobile home and loaded everything we owned onto a truck. When we moved in with everything we had, you could still hear echoes. We certainly had a lot more room in the residence than we had in the mobile home. The house itself had a nearly full-size basement, four bedrooms, a den, a living room, two bathrooms, a dining room, kitchen, and a large attic with pull-down stairs. There was a large garden space, a very sizable lawn, and my office door was only about a hundred feet from the back door of the house.

The residence at French Creek was quite an
improvement over a mobile home on a small lot.

* * *

French Creek Game Farm was just what the name implied. It had been established in the 1920s for the purpose of rearing game birds to release around the state to bolster declining populations. Over the years, it became obvious that pen-raised birds and game animals lacked the "wildness" to have much effect on wild populations, and the game farm gradually evolved into a menagerie where people could come to view animals and birds that had become rare in the state. Over time, species were added as attractions for the public, and the game farm became the closest thing to a zoo in the whole state. There was even an African lion, some peafowl, and various other exotic game birds like golden and silver pheasants from Asia. The lion had died from a kidney infection only a few months before I arrived and, after some discussion, a decision was made to exhibit only animals and birds that are, or once were, native to West Virginia. These included (in descending order, by size) bison, elk, black bears, white-tailed deer, mountain lions, timber wolves, bobcats, red and gray foxes, raccoons, opossums, groundhog, fox and gray squirrels, and other small mammals when they were available. Among the birds on display were eagles, owls, hawks, wild turkeys, and various game birds.

The need for realistic habitat exhibits had not yet become the norm, and most of the animals were displayed in cages that had been there for many years. Most of those cages had cement floors which were hosed down daily to keep them clean and some form of shelter from the hot sun or inclement weather. By modern zoo standards, those animal displays would be considered primitive and unacceptable, but we made do with what we had and hoped for something better.

The game farm property had once been a dairy farm, situated about twelve miles south of Buckhannon, West Virginia, and bisected by state routes 4 and 20. Most of the more than 300 acres lie along a ridgeline at about 1,800 feet in elevation. There was a large barn, a smaller milking house, a two-story frame building which housed an office/shop/garage, four smaller frame buildings which had been brooder houses, and the residence all on the west side of the highway. The exhibit area and the District III office building which had offices for forestry, wildlife, law enforcement, water resources, and fisheries was on the east side of the highway. There was also a small gift shop and a couple of parking lots. Feeding the animals, cleaning the exhibits, and maintaining the area seven days a week was a challenge for a crew of only five or six men. We all had plenty to keep us busy.

* * *

There were a couple of aspects of this new job that I had not anticipated or even considered. First, over the years, the game farm had become the repository of many of the sick, injured, or orphaned animals or birds that the public happened to come across. These included everything from fawns to bear cubs to little raccoons to flying squirrels and from eagles to hawks to owls to robins and wrens. The expectation was that we could rehabilitate anything and either put it on exhibit or release it back to the wild. Of course, this was frequently impossible due to the poor condition of the animals when we received them. Although it was not legal for a private citizen to possess this wildlife, they were very seldom prosecuted because their intentions were honorable. Some, however, were prosecuted because their intention was obviously to keep the animal for a pet. The most common of the "foundling orphans" were white-tailed deer fawns. In most of these incidents, the following scenario played out: Mom, Dad, and the kids are driving along a country road, they come around a bend, and there is a fawn in the road ahead. The fawn goes into the roadside ditch and lies down motionless with its head down (its natural defense). The car pulls alongside and stops. "Oh, isn't it beautiful." "Maybe it's hurt." "I wonder where its mother is." They all look around and don't see an adult deer. (Of course they don't because the doe is nearby and staying hidden.) "Dad, can we take it home and keep it?" "Something must have happened to its mother!" "It will die if we don't take care of it." So they gather it up and take it into the car. On the way home, they pet and play with it. A young fawn is essentially fearless, and when nothing bad happens, it will respond in almost the same way it would to its mother by nosing around and seeking to nurse. There is nothing more endearing (pun intended) than a young fawn. After about a week, word gets around that the family has a pet deer, conservation officers hear about it, confiscate it, and bring it to the game farm. It arrives with no fear of humans and usually a severe case of diarrhea. Along with forty or fifty other fawns, it is now a problem deer.

Lori holds a small fox pup. All infant animals are cute, but like human babies, they grow up.

The second aspect was that it had become traditional for the game farm to provide wildlife exhibits for fairs, festivals, and other public gatherings all over West Virginia. It seemed that every town in the state had an annual fair or festival of some type, and they all requested an exhibit to add another attraction to their event. Besides, lots of West Virginians were interested in wildlife. They liked to hunt and fish, and we didn't charge any fees to bring an exhibit. We felt that DNR exposure was a plus. However, honoring an exhibit request put a real strain on our staff. To deliver and set up an exhibit required two men, several cages, a large truck, several animals, food, water, bedding for the animals, a full day each way to set up and load up and return home. For a two-day event, someone had to man the exhibit to answer questions and ensure safety for the animals and the public. All this required a bare minimum of six man/days per event, and many of those days were twelve hours instead of eight.

In addition to feeding animals, cleaning exhibits, mowing grass, collecting trash, and other routine chores, our crew was constantly confronted by little problems that needed solutions. Equipment would break. Keys would be locked inside a car in the parking lot. A toilet in the restroom would overflow. Someone would bring in a new baby animal. A waterline would spring a leak. Someone would have a flat tire. People from the district divisions were always coming and going. We were never bored, and we had a good crew!

CHAPTER X

The Crew

THE CREW AT the game farm was an interesting group of men. Though their backgrounds were varied, they all had several things in common. They were rural West Virginia men who loved to hunt and fish. They had a good work ethic, were familiar with outdoor skills, and would approach every job with a "git-'er-done" attitude. Collectively, they knew how to do a surprising range of things from auto mechanics to building fence to plumbing to carpentry to basic electrical work to roofing and cement work. Together we could tackle almost any job that came along.

Clyde Campbell was my assistant. He had been an auto mechanic and a state trapper (predator and rabies control). About ten years my senior, he was a hard worker and after some years of being on the move all over the state, he liked the idea of staying at home. He is still the most accomplished hunter I have ever known. In ensuing years, Clyde and I would share some real adventures. More about that later.

Robbie Cutright, a fellow Vietnam veteran, was a conservation aide. He had grown up on a farm, was a willing and energetic worker, and though short and mild mannered, had forearms like Popeye and strength well beyond his small stature. He would later become a valued wildlife manager for the DNR.

Danny Reed, also a local farm boy, was Mr. Dependable. No matter how bad the roads became in winter, he would be there whenever he was scheduled even though he had to drive more than twenty miles. Danny was very quiet and low-key, but he had a great sense of dry humor. He was very patient and thorough, and if it had a motor, he could get it running again. After several months, I was shocked to discover that he is also a first-rate banjo player who can hear a tune two or three times and then play it like a professional. You'd never know because he never talked about it.

We also employed three or four men as seasonal or temporary workers, and we had one or two Neighborhood Youth Corps crews, each with a supervisor, who could help with special projects for six to eight weeks in the summer. Though most of the NYC work was menial, it did help the game farm look better.

A couple of the men on the labor payroll were noteworthy: John Howard and Theron Smallridge. John could be well described as "a little rough around the edges!" He was forty-something and a bear of a man who was strong as an ox. His life had not been easy, and he was accustomed to being talked down to or disregarded and disrespected. I decided that he should be regarded with the same dignity and respect as anyone else, and I would ask his opinion just the same as I would ask others. I discovered that his response was loyalty and extreme effort to please. He took pride in his work and was diligent in performing the most mundane tasks to the best of his ability and after a few encouraging words, would spare no effort to get the job done. In the spring, usually March, we would have a roundup of bottle-raised fawns, draw blood samples to ensure they were disease free, and ship them to areas of the state with very low deer populations. The fawn pen was equipped with staging pens and a smooth-sided loading chute that had a small side door. The process was to catch all the fawns, which were now fifty to sixty pounds, draw blood samples, ear-tag them, and release them back into the pen. When blood work indicated they were good to go, they were loaded into big boxes, transported, and released. The problem with deer is that they became totally fractious when pressed, so getting them out of the loading chute to draw blood could be an absolute rodeo. I would call on John to catch deer and bring them out. He would go in the side door and after much crashing, banging, and swearing, he would always emerge from the side door with a deer in each hand and a firm grip on both hind legs. Though muddied, bloodied, and panting from exertion, he was very proud of the fact that he could catch deer quicker and with less damage than anyone else.

John knew that I was an avid grouse hunter, and one Monday morning, he proudly announced that he had killed a grouse on Saturday. I suspected that he might have sluiced it along a back road somewhere, so I said, "Really? Did you shoot it on the wing?"

His response was, "Hell no. I shot 'im all over!"

Theron Smallridge was one of those people whom, once exposed to, you will never forget. He was young, just recently out of high school, where I'm sure he was a frustration and exasperation to every teacher he had because he had no regard for anything that happened in a classroom. His total focus was on the outdoors. He could imitate any sound with astonishing clarity, and he was the most ingenious practical joker I have ever known.

The office/shop building had two restrooms, one out in the shop and one built into the corner of the office. One day, Clyde and I were doing paperwork in the office when Theron burst through the door and said, "Man, I'm bustin' to pee, and someone's in the other john." He bolted into the restroom, slammed the door, and very soon, we could hear liquid splashing into the toilet bowl. (That room wasn't exactly soundproof.) The splashing went on, and on, and on, and on. Finally, Clyde and I looked at each other with raised eyebrows, and Clyde went over and opened the door. There stood Theron with a big grin carefully pouring water into the bowl from a five-gallon bucket. He said, "I was wondering how long it would take you guys to see if I needed help!"

* * *

We had a two-ton dump truck with heavy sideboards and tailgate made from oak lumber. Clyde took Theron with him to town to get a load of gravel to patch our roads. Theron could help him with the heavy tailgate. There is only one straight stretch in the twelve miles where it's safe to pass another vehicle with a dump truck. Just before they got to the straight, they came upon a slow-moving VW van. When Clyde could see far enough ahead, he pulled out to pass, and the van sped up. He kept the throttle floored and could still hear the van straining along beside him. As he neared the end of the straight, they were almost up to seventy. In a slight curve, he finally picked up the van in the mirror. It was far behind them and Theron was sitting on the passenger side making noises that sounded exactly like a racing VW!

One night, we had a skunk dig its way into our quail exhibit and kill several birds. Theron came to me and vowed to catch that skunk. He said, "I've heard that if you snatch a skunk off the ground by the tail, that it can't spray you. Is that true?"

I said, "I don't know, but I wouldn't try it."

A couple of days later, he had his chance and did try it. The skunk sprayed him right in the face, and he was temporarily blinded. We got him into the bed of a pickup and drove him to the emergency room at the local hospital. They would not let him near the ER door but made him stand outside on the lawn and hosed him down with a garden hose from about twenty-five to thirty feet away. By the next morning, his vision was fine, but the odor persisted for two or three days. That episode certainly dispelled another rumor.

CHAPTER XI

The Animals

ONE OF OUR most perplexing and time-consuming jobs at the game farm was the care and feeding of white-tailed deer fawns. It was not unusual for us to receive thirty to seventy fawns each spring, and it seemed that everyone had theories on how they should be handled and fed. Though we tried to keep an open mind about all these theories, it soon became apparent that greater attention to detail was needed to ensure the best survival rate. Most of the fawns came to us with problems resulting from improper feeding. The wrong milk formula or the wrong amount or frequency can cause the stomach bacteria to malfunction which leads to diarrhea, dehydration, and fever. The fawn would die. Though we tried treating the symptoms with antibiotics and Kaopectate, we still lost fawns. We decided to go back to the source, the doe.

Feeding fawns became a lot of work. Some years we had as many as seventy to feed and care for three times each day.

We caught and milked a lactating doe (that was a real rodeo, and we only got about three ounces of milk, but that was enough to analyze) and discovered that deer milk is far higher in fat and protein than the richest Guernsey milk. It was also discovered that the fat globules in the milk are so small that cream does not rise to the top; the deer milk is naturally homogenized. The only domestic animal that produces similar milk is a dairy goat, so we found a lady with dairy goats and began to purchase almost all her goats' milk.

In a natural situation, a doe will normally have two fawns. She will visit them only three or four times in a twenty-four-hour period and nurse them, groom them, and lick their behinds to stimulate defecation and urination. Then she will leave them to lie quietly while she goes to feed and rest separately. The best defense for the young fawns is lack of scent and movement and their natural camouflage. They are also seldom right together so that a single predator cannot get them both. When they do nurse, they only get about five or six ounces of milk at a time. When they are strong and fleet enough to keep up with the doe, they will accompany her until they are weaned and go on to breed and produce fawns of their own. Even then, they may remain in a family group for generations with the oldest doe as the leader. This behavior pattern ensures that young deer are not indiscriminately exposed to interactions with other family groups from different habitats. (They aren't crowded together with a bunch of strangers.) This is one of nature's mechanisms to ensure the health and well-being of local deer herds.

Our problem was that fawns came to us from all over the state, and it was impossible to isolate each one of them. The best we could do was to quarantine any fawn that appeared sick or scoured and treat it individually. All the others were fed three times a day with sterilized bottles and nipples. They were groomed and evaluated at each feeding, and defecation was stimulated with a wet sponge. They were then released into a holding pen (approximately one acre) until it was time for the next feeding. There was no way we could prevent the licking, nuzzling, and exchange of slobbers that occur among dozens of fawns. Although it required a tremendous amount of work, our fawn survival rate improved dramatically, and we were able to restock several areas in the state that had not had many deer for decades.

* * *

White-tailed deer are the most popular and sought-after species of big game in North America. As such, they are the subject of a great deal of interest and the object of a huge amount of research. We have learned more about whitetails in the last fifty years than any other game species. We have studied the habitat, behavior, habits, biology, chemistry, reproduction, social structure, and even the acuity of the senses of whitetails. They are beautiful, graceful, elusive, and delicious. They have a high rate of reproduction which allows a heavy harvest, and they can bounce back quickly from a year of high mortality. They are the ultimate big game animal. Millions of dollars are spent on research to learn more about deer, and many more millions are spent each year in their pursuit. The operative word here is DOLLARS.

Americans have always been quick to sniff out the potential for profit from anything that is popular. We are also quite gullible about buying anything that promises instant success. We want positive results, and we want them NOW! This attitude has resulted in an explosive proliferation of gadgets, gizmos, widgets, and whatnots that we just cannot hunt deer without. We must have full camo, an ATV, the latest rifle/caliber, rattling horns, grunt call, trail cameras, portable tree stands, ground blinds, rubber boots, etc. Of course, we must have scent killer for ourselves and doe-in-heat urine to attract the buck we hope to see. While most of these new products have a minimal impact on deer biology, the widespread use of deer scent products gives me cause for real concern. The only conditions where the raw materials used to make these products can be obtained are conditions where deer are closely contained or crowded and under stress. They are frequently unsanitary and subject to the coming and going of individual deer from various sources.

There is a disease called Chronic Wasting Disease (CWD), which is thought to originate in these conditions, and it is fatal to every infected deer. CWD is caused by a mutated protein called a prion which can remain infectious in the environment for years. There is no known test to detect CWD in live deer, and there is no treatment or cure. CWD is transmitted through saliva, urine, feces, and other body secretions and can be picked up by healthy deer merely by browsing or bedding down in an area where infected deer have been.

Because of the potential for introducing CWD into a local healthy deer herd and because of the possibility of catastrophic effects, I would strongly object to the use of any attractant, scent, or calming agent that contains any animal products or by-products. Nature has fine-tuned all animals to fit nicely and naturally into their environment. That process has probably taken thousands of years, and the tinkerings of man with genetics, biology, chemistry, and behavior are not likely to improve the situation in only two or three decades. It would be better to enjoy and appreciate our natural wildlife resources than to make mistakes in trying to modify them for our own profit or bragging purposes.

* * *

Another species that we soon became quite familiar with was the black bear, the West Virginia state animal. I'm not sure just how citizens came into possession of a bear cub, but every year, we would have some bear cubs brought to us. This usually happened about the time of spring gobbler season or when ramp diggers were out and about in the woods. The probable scenario was that a hunter or ramp digger would come across a bear cub in the woods, collect it, and bring it home. The mother bear was probably nearby, but her fear of man was stronger than her maternal instinct, and she would not attack to defend her cub. Cubs are born in a winter den usually in January or February, and they weigh only a few ounces and are blind and hairless at birth. While mother and cubs are in the den, the cubs nurse and grow. By the time spring arrives, the cubs have grown to about two pounds and look like miniature adults. When plants begin to emerge and grow, mama bear comes out of the den in search of food, and the cubs come with her. They will follow her and learn what things are good to eat though they still continue to nurse.

Now bears are nowhere near as delicate as fawns in their eating requirements, and they can eat and digest a variety of foods without developing intestinal problems. By May or June, they are still nursing, but they are experimenting with solid foods and doing quite well. We usually received them in April or early May when they still needed to nurse. We would bring them into the residence where it was warmer, and we could bottle-feed them and keep an eye on them to make sure they were okay. Shelia was wonderful about all this and she would wash and sterilize bottles, help with feeding, and offer maternal insight. (It actually helps to burp a bear cub after it nurses.) Then she would put them out in the lawn to pee and poop, play with them for a bit, and then tuck them into a big blanket-lined cardboard box that we kept in the basement near the furnace where it was warm. Often, we would turn them loose in the basement where they could run and play and climb without getting into trouble.

Shelia and I serve lunch in the kitchen for a pair of bear cubs

Shelia's maternal instincts were a real asset
in the caring for small animals.

There were single cubs that I will always remember. One was a little male that Shelia called Pep because he always seemed to have lots of energy. She would bring him up to the kitchen while she was working there, and he would play and snoop around until he would tire and lie down and go to sleep on the kitchen floor. Many times, Shelia would want something from the garden and she would say, "Come on, Pep. Let's go get some beans or tomatoes." She'd walk out the back door and across the lawn to the garden about a hundred yards away with Pep following right along behind her. When she got what she wanted, she'd say, "Come on, Pep. Let's go to the house," and Pep would follow all the way back into the kitchen. No coaching or leading was necessary, as he tagged along just like he would have with his mother.

The other cub was a male that we fed morning, noon, and evening, but that wasn't enough. After his evening meal, we'd put him to bed in the basement box. The problem was that after everyone upstairs was in bed asleep, the slightest sound would awaken him, and he would climb out of the box, up the stairs to the kitchen door, and squall bloody murder until he got something to eat. I would get up, put on an old terry cloth bathrobe, and go to the kitchen where I'd get a bottle out of the refrigerator and warm it in the microwave. Then I'd sit down by the door and reach up to open it. Instantly I'd have a hungry black fur ball on my chest wanting to be fed. After feeding and burping him, I'd put him back to bed and we were good until morning. Shelia said, "You never got up with the kids when they cried at night."

I replied, "The kids never squalled that loud!"

Sometimes people would refer to me as Poppa Bear!
Photo by Steven Rotsch

* * *

There was one little cub that we were keeping in a cage in the shop. Theron came to me and said that the cub needed to have some sunshine, so we put a small dog collar on him and tethered him out in the backyard on a swivel. He did not like being restrained and soon pulled back hard enough to pop the collar over his head, and across the yard he went. Our yard was encircled by some very large white pine trees and, as soon as the cub got to one, up he went almost to the very top. Theron said, "I'll climb up there and shake him out," so I ran into the house and got a blanket to catch him with. Four of us stood under the tree holding the corners of the blanket. Theron went up that tree like a monkey, and I began to worry that those brittle small pine limbs wouldn't hold him, but true to his word, he did manage to get close enough to the cub to shake him out, and we caught him in the blanket forty feet below. We tightened up the collar, put it back on the cub, and tethered him out again. In less than two minutes, the cub was loose again and the same scenario played out, only this time it was a different tree, and the cub was taken back to his cage in the shop.

Just imagine shaking this little rascal out of a
tree and catching him in a blanket.
Photo by Steven Rotsch

Another time, we had brought a cub into the house and were keeping it in a cardboard box by the kitchen refrigerator where the motor kept it warm. At the time, we had a miniature toy poodle that was a pet for our two daughters. Shelia was teaching, the kids were in school, and Buffy (the poodle) was the daytime master of the house. One time at noon, I went to the house for lunch, and I noticed that the fold down lid on the box was open. At the same time, I heard growling coming from the living room. I went in to find the cub on the top of my recliner with its ears laid back, its upper lip sticking out, and showing a very belligerent attitude. The little dog was pacing around the chair growling up at the cub. I fed the bear, took him and his box to the basement, and restored the proper order. Thereafter, I told people that the little dog was my bear dog and that she could tree a bear with the best of them.

* * *

One spring, we received a total of thirteen bear cubs, and we began to recognize what a wide range of personalities these cubs had. One was a complete "teddy bear" with a sweet and gentle disposition. He would climb up your leg to get into a feeding position and then flop over onto his back to be held and given a bottle. He seemed to enjoy being cuddled, and he never exhibited anger or aggression. At the other end of the spectrum was a cub that was always biting, scratching, or getting into a fight with his peers. All the rest were somewhere in between, but we soon learned that each of them was pretty predictable in behavior and needed to be handled accordingly. We also learned to read the nuances of body language, and we all knew that you just didn't mess with a bear whose upper lip was protruding.

Of course, we didn't have the facilities to keep all these bears, so we had to find a way to dispose of them. There is nothing cuter than a bear cub, except two or three of them together, and so we were often able to find a home for them in zoos or wildlife parks like Busch Gardens or Disney World. Even this did not solve the too-many-bears problem, so we began to foster them out to mother bears who were still in their dens with cubs. We (the DNR bear study program) had several sows with radio collars that could be located in their dens. We could go to a bear den and add another cub or two to the naturally born cubs that the mother bear had produced. The method of doing this was to tranquilize the sow, examine her cubs, rub a little Vicks salve on the mother's nose and all the cubs (we'd add one or two), reverse the tranquilizer, and leave as quickly and quietly as possible. The great thing about mother bears is that they can't count. They don't seem to recognize that they now have more cubs than before, and they treat them all the same. They are wonderful mothers and exhibit more patience and perseverance than anyone might expect.

We once had a sow with two cubs that were in a holding pen on the back side of the game farm. We decided to introduce a particularly obnoxious cub to see if she could settle it down and get it to behave like the other two. Although the new cub would squall, bite, and scratch, she never lost patience with it and she was gentle and tender with it as she tried to draw it to her breast to nurse. She finally succeeded after about a week, and that cub did finally settle down. The way he acted at first, I'd have cuffed him all over that pen. We were all impressed by what a great mother that bear was.

* * *

When I arrived at the game farm, there was a black bear exhibit that was essentially a concrete-floored cage that was in a prominent location at the top of a hill and very close to the gift shop. There were usually a big male and two smaller females in that exhibit. The male in residence was called "Tobe" and he was indeed a large bear (approaching 450 lbs.). Do Not Feed the Animals was still not in vogue, and being near the gift shop, Tobe was regularly fed sodas, peanuts, and popcorn through the chain-link fence of the cage. It was fascinating to watch this big bear take a bag of peanuts, lie down with the peanuts between his front paws, and eat them one at a time with the shells dribbling from the sides of his mouth and never a nut wasted. This was done with the delicacy and precision of a talented artist. He also drank copious amounts of soda, probably gallons per day, but he would never drink diet soda. He would snort and turn away from all diet drinks. When he died at an old age, I suspected it was from diabetes.

CHAPTER XII

Life at French Creek

ONLY A FEW days after I began work at the game farm, a very distinguished-looking gentleman walked into my office. He had white hair, dark-rimmed glasses, and a deep, clear voice.

He said, "I came to meet you and let you know who I am. My name is John Weimer. I'm a veterinarian, and I live in Buckhannon. I work for the state Department of Agriculture."

We shook hands, I offered him a seat, and we talked for several minutes.

Finally, I said, "Well, Dr. Weimer, what can I do for you today?"

Very calmly, he replied, "I was wondering if you could have your men build me a dog box for the back of my truck."

I thought about it for a moment, looked him squarely in the eyes, and said, "Why the hell should I?"

Still very calm, he said, "Well, I've done a good bit of work on the animals here, and I suppose I could submit a bill for my time and the drugs and materials I've used in the last few months."

That really gave me something to think about. (I knew that vet bills could be quite expensive, and a homemade dog box wasn't a big deal.)

I replied, "You know, Dr. Weimer, I think we can build you a dog box."

He said, "Please call me John."

I think we each had just passed our first inspection of the other.

John and I became the best of friends and outdoor companions because we had a lot in common. We had both grown up on small farms. He had served in the army in Burma in World War II, and I had served in Vietnam. We both loved bird hunting and bird dogs, and we often hunted together in West Virginia and several other states. Our views on politics, education, and the outdoors were similar. He may have learned a few things from me, and I learned a lot from him. He was the most direct and to the point person I have ever known, and his use of words and choice of phrases were often so memorable that a mutual friend and I began to refer to them as "Weimerisms." For example: John and I were on a hunting trip, and I was driving when we came to a T intersection. I stopped and looked both ways. Nothing was coming from the left, and a pickup truck was coming from the right. I signaled and started to turn right when suddenly the pickup turned sharply to his left and cut me off so badly that I had to run off the road to avoid being hit. I said loudly, "Lay over there, you *sob!*" It was cold and the windows were up. We drove on down the road for a couple of miles, and John looked over at me and said, "Bill, one of these days you're going to encounter a big, mean, tough, pugnacious deaf-mute who can read lips!" That was a classic Weimerism.

* * *

One fall evening, I had a small bear (large cub) brought in that had been hit by a vehicle. I could tell that a back leg was broken, so I called John. He said to bring her in and we'd get an X-ray and see if she could be fixed. The X-ray showed a shattered femur, and John said we'd have to amputate the leg. I wasn't sure she could survive, but we removed the leg anyway. We kept her for several months, and John would come by often to check on her. Her called her Orphan Annie, and I called her Tripod. She never lost her feisty disposition, and she regained mobility and appetite. We released her into the wild that next summer. Five years later, she was killed by an archery hunter, and placental scars indicated that she had birthed at least two pairs of cubs.

John taught me how to draw blood from deer so we could have all deer to be released checked for brucellosis and other diseases which could affect livestock. Our state Department of Agriculture was very helpful and cooperative in this process, and we never had a deer test positive for disease. This was a proactive process to prevent any claims that livestock became infected from deer that we had released.

We kept a small group of bison for display in a four-acre paddock area. Bison were once native to West Virginia but not in large herds. They were eastern woodland bison that roamed the area in smaller family groups of six to ten animals. When the group moved from place to place, they would create trails which were used by Indians. Later, early settlers would enlarge these trails until they became roads. Since the bison would always follow the path of least resistance, it is quite probable that today many of the state's secondary roads were once "buffalo trails."

* * *

Our exhibit usually included a bull and four or five cows. One Sunday afternoon (these things always seemed to occur on weekends), the guys came to me and said that one of the cows was having a calf and she seemed to be having trouble. I called John and he said he'd be right out. By the time he arrived, the cow had expelled the calf but also the entire reproductive tract. This is known as a prolapsed uterus, which countryfolk call "throwing the calf bed." The only remedy is to physically reinsert it and administer heavy doses of antibiotics. I tranquilized her with a dart gun, and we got to work putting her back together. When we finished, we were standing there trying to wipe some of the mess off our hands and arms with paper towels when I looked up to see the bull charging with his head down, tail up, and malice in his attitude, grunting with every step.

I shouted, "Look out, John!" John whirled and threw a roll of paper towels which struck the bull right between the eyes. The bull recoiled so violently that his butt actually hit the ground. He whirled and thundered away, much to our relief. I said, "John, with a fast ball like that, you could make a lot of money in the majors." We both laughed and retreated outside the paddock to monitor the cow in safety.

* * *

It was fairly common for people to bring us sick or injured animals in hopes that we could rehabilitate and release them. One evening, someone brought in an adult female golden eagle that was obviously injured and unable to fly. I immediately called John, described what I had, and requested his help. The X-rays clearly showed about seven or eight large shot pellets, mostly in the wings and legs but one or two in the body. With small incisions and a probe, we were able to remove all but the two in the body. There were no broken bones, and we decided to leave those two and concentrate on rehab with plenty of food and antibiotics. Over the next several weeks, she recovered nicely, and we would fly her on a tethering cord until she was strong and adept enough to catch her own food. When she had become capable enough to be released, we decided to take her to Blackwater Falls State Park and release her over the Blackwater Canyon during Wildflower Weekend, an event hosted by the State Parks. The attendees were mostly nature lovers who were bused in from cities along the east coast and included several members of the Audubon Society and Sierra Club.

The release was scheduled for 9:00 AM. We had the eagle in a covered cage, and I was to bring her out for leg banding, photo ops, and the release. I put on a pair of heavy welder's gloves, eased into the cage, and was very careful to grab both feet. (If one of those feet should grab you, it would inflict a severe wound.) As I was backing out of the cage, paying careful attention to those talons, she obviously decided she'd had enough of me and bit me through the ear. As I stood there through the leg banding and picture taking, my ear was dripping blood on my freshly ironed uniform shirt. A young man approached, took pictures, and said, "That is really cool to have your ear pierced by an eagle." I replied, "If you think that's cool, just lean over here and we'll fix you right up!" He declined (the coward), and the release was a big hit.

It's appropriate to note here that predators have the ability to exert tremendous force when closing down their killing stroke. Canines, felines, and birds of prey can close down their teeth or talons with thousands of pounds of pressure per square inch. However, the muscles and tendons which open the jaws or talons are relatively weak, allowing them to be kept closed with very little pressure. In other words, once I got those talons folded closed in my hand, the eagle could not open them up. Had she been able to close down on my hand or arm, those sharp talons could easily have penetrated completely through.

* * *

One day, we were going through the routine of vaccinating the exhibit animals. John was there to administer the shots, and he and I both agreed that the best method of handling shots was to physically subdue the animal as quickly as possible, give it its shots, and release it. This resulted in less stress and trauma for the animal than to use drugs to immobilize it. To do this, we had "squeeze" cages that enabled us to mash an animal against bars where the shots could be given quickly, followed by an immediate release. The trick was getting the animal into the squeeze cage. We had fashioned a hoop net with a large iron ring, three layers of heavy burlap, and a long handle. We could scoop up an animal, flip the "net" over, and dump him into the squeeze cage. One bobcat decided he didn't want to play that game, and he was flying around his cage like a giant pinball. I scooped him off the wall as he went by and started to dump him into the squeeze cage. I was wearing a pair of heavy welder's gloves. He latched onto the sack and wouldn't let go, so I grabbed the bottom of the sack to shake him out. Instantly, he bit through the sack, the welder's glove, and my thumbnail right to the quick. Almost fifty years later, I am still reminded of the power of a predator's bite by looking at my disfigured thumbnail.

* * *

Another interesting characteristic of predators is that they always attack prey by surprise from above or behind. A predator will not make a frontal assault unless it is threatened and there is no apparent escape. Like all animals, predators must survive, reproduce, and avoid serious injury in the process. Although they have evolved to kill and eat other animals, they will do so only when they have a distinct advantage and there is very little chance of serious injury to themselves. This behavior is instinctive and was clearly illustrated by an incident which happened in our basement.

We had a young mountain lion that we were keeping in the basement of the house where we would feed it, pet it, and play with it. It was only a little larger than an average house cat, still eating milk, and, as many young mammals are, quite playful and cute. Shelia and I had just fed the cat and were sitting on an old couch, watching it play and explore the room. From time to time, we would make eye contact with it, and it was obviously in a playful mood. Shelia got to playing peekaboo with it over the back of the couch, and I said, "You'd better be careful!" When Shelia ducked down, the cat flew across the room, sailed over the back of the couch, and landed with all four feet on Shelia's head. That was not an attack but play guided by instinct to prepare that mountain lion for the rigors of adulthood. The elements of speed and surprise were highlighted here—especially for Shelia!

This little mountain lion taught Shelia a
lesson about speed and surprise.

* * *

A photographer had persuaded me to grant him access to the great horned owl cage so that he could get some clear and unobstructed pictures. We had even fashioned a perch and an appropriate background. Three times the photographer kept getting closer while snapping away. Three times the owl bailed out and tried to escape. Three times I caught him and put him back on the perch. (I was wearing heavy welders gloves.) The fourth time he bailed, he was on the ground backed into a corner. As I approached, he suddenly leaped at me with talons extended and grabbed at my eyes. I got cuts on both eyebrows and both cheeks. Had I not been wearing glasses I could have been blinded. I told the photographer, "We're done here," and we left the cage. The moral of this little story is that all predators will attack when cornered. They have no empathy, they have no conscience, and they certainly have no sense of fair play. They have evolved to inflict damage, to kill, and to survive all encounters.

* * *

One aspect of life at French Creek that could sometimes become problematic was keeping all the animals properly fed. For the most part, herbivores took care of themselves (except for the bottle-feeding of the very young) and did quite well with grazing, supplemental hay, prepared livestock feed, and availability of salt and minerals. Carnivores and omnivores, on the other hand, could be difficult because of their need for a varied diet. In addition to meat, they needed compounds found in hair, bones, and internal organs such as heart, lungs, kidneys, pancreas, and stomach. We needed about forty to fifty pounds of fresh meat each day to feed mountain lions, bobcats, wolves, foxes, hawks, eagles, and owls. Although it was possible to buy meat, what was available was expensive and often of poor quality. Thus we adopted a policy of picking up all the road-killed animals that we could reasonably get to. Word soon got around that a call to me or our office would result in a roadkill being picked up quickly while it was still fresh. These were brought back to the game farm where we would feed the animals fresh meat or cut, wrap, and freeze it for future use.

Since deer move the most very early and very late in the day, I got a lot of calls at home when the office was closed. I would go to retrieve the animal, hang and skin it, and leave it hanging for the men to cut up the next day. I skinned a lot of deer and got pretty adept at it. I learned a lot about deer anatomy and how to disassemble one and efficiently use the meat.

Over the years, I've pulled more than 1,000 deer up into the bed of a pickup truck. If I never need to do it again, I will not object.

Later on, I would give public demonstrations on how to properly field dress, skin, and butcher a deer so that successful hunters could achieve maximum use of a valuable resource.

I do a public demonstration on field dressing,
skinning and butchering a deer so that successful
hunters can better utilize a valuable resource.

* * *

When you literally "live on the job," there will be times when you're confronted with unforeseen problems. One Sunday afternoon, a boy of eight to ten years old came to the door and asked if I could use a copperhead for our snake exhibit. I said, "Sure. Do you have a copperhead?"

He said, "Yes, and it's a big one!"

I said, "Where do you have it?"

He said, "My buddy's got it out there at the edge of the yard!"

I walked out to the other boy who was holding a three-foot copperhead firmly behind the head in a very professional grip. The three of us walked over to the snake exhibit where the holder released his charge, and I snapped the lock back in place.

I said, "Where did you boys learn to catch snakes?"

The holder said, "We watched 'em do it with forked sticks on *Wild Kingdom*."

I asked, "Do your mothers know you're doing this?"

They said, "No. You won't tell, will you?"

I said, "No," and I didn't.
Until now.

* * *

Another warm Sunday afternoon, a car sped into the driveway, screeched to a stop, and a woman jumped out and ran toward the house yelling "Help! Help me! I left my dog in the car, and I think he's dying." One look at the dog confirmed that it was indeed suffering from heat stroke. The breathing was rapid and shallow. The dog was not responsive. I quickly laid the dog in a wheelbarrow with its nose up and started running water over its body with a garden hose. While my daughters ran to the house for ice and the woman continued with the garden hose, I called the nearest vet clinic. A few minutes later, the woman sped off toward the clinic with her dog wrapped in an old blanket with ice. A few days later, I got a very nice thank you note in the mail. The dog had survived and recovered nicely.

When we first moved to the game farm, our two daughters, Lori (4) and Lisa (1) were very small, and Shelia wanted to stay at home until both girls were in school. That turned out very well, as all four of us had much to learn about a wide variety of animals and birds. By the time both girls were in elementary school and Shelia had returned to teaching fourth grade, we all had a much better idea of how to care for small animals. Both girls became adept at bottle-feeding young mammals and were quite comfortable around cubs, fawns, small raccoons, squirrels, rabbits, woodchucks, etc. They were always willing to help whenever they could. By the time they were in high school and middle school, they were also adept at answering the phone, taking messages, and getting explicit directions to the location of a road-killed deer.

Our two girls, Lori left and Lisa right, soon became
adept at helping care for small animals.

It became apparent that our house was the preferred location
for teenage get-togethers. We had plenty of parking space, a quiet
location, a big TV with a VCR, and parents who would take the little
dog to their bedroom and let them have the living room for movies.

Besides, where else could you play with a bear cub and a soccer
ball or share your movie popcorn with a little raccoon?

Usually, the kids would pause the movie about midway and hit
the kitchen for snacks. Immediately, our little dog would be scratching at the bedroom door to be let out. When the snacks were gone,
she would be back at the door, scratching to come back in. I made
the observation, "That little dog can hear the crash and thunder of
Saran Wrap coming off a snack bowl from more than a mile away."

All four of us in our family liked and very much enjoyed all the
little animals, but Lisa was the one who became the "animal whisperer."
She loved every one of them, and it was amazing to watch her establish
a rapport with them, and it was obvious that they loved her too.

We had a small bobcat kitten that we bottle-fed, and each of us
would take turns feeding and playing with her. We called her Kitty.

(Not very original, I'll admit.) Lisa and Kitty spent a lot of time together, and when Kitty was about half-grown they would go outside and play hide-and-seek. Lisa would slip off around the corner of the house, and Kitty would slink to the corner and peek around. When she saw Lisa, she would dash to her and leap up to be caught at chest height. These episodes would end with Lisa laughing and cuddling Kitty, and Kitty purring like an idling lawnmower.

Before long though, Kitty had grown big enough, and her claws were sharp enough to draw blood from everyone, except Lisa, who tried to play with her. Since we planned for her to be an exhibit animal, I decided to have her declawed while we were on vacation. When we returned, Shelia and Lisa went to pick her up from the vet clinic. The clinic staff thought that Kitty was the most vicious animal they'd ever dealt with, and they were astonished when Lisa calmly opened the cage door and, purring loudly, Kitty walked out into her arms.

Lisa, whom we called our animal whisperer,
cuddles Kitty and comforts a bear cub.

* * *

The wide variety of people I met and the diversity of tasks that I needed to get accomplished always kept me fully engaged in my job. This morning I might give a couple of tours for third and fourth graders. This afternoon might find me helping install a new hydraulic cylinder on a dump truck. Tomorrow I might meet with the architect to review the blueprints for a new exhibit, give a talk at a Rotary luncheon, and explain to a little old lady how to keep the raccoons out of her garbage can. The next day I might pick up a couple of road-killed deer, check some fecal samples for the presence of parasites, fix a leaking commode in the picnic area, explain DNR policies and procedures to a couple of hunters headed for deer camp, and host a group of professors who were visiting nearby West Virginia Wesleyan College. Every day brought new challenges, and I was never bored. I loved my job!

CHAPTER XIII

More Animal Stories

ONE AFTERNOON IN late January, my office phone rang, and the caller identified himself as Skip Johnson. Skip was the outdoor writer for the *Charleston Gazette* newspaper and covered many subjects of interest to West Virginians who like to hunt, fish, or pursue outdoor activities. Skip's column was widely read, and he had developed a very good reputation for accuracy and thoroughness. He wanted to come to the game farm, possibly get a picture of a groundhog, and interview me about groundhog biology. I agreed and we set up a time.

A couple of days later, Skip showed up and we sat and talked groundhog for over an hour. Skip asked if we had a weather forecasting groundhog, and I said, "Of course!" He asked if the forecasts were accurate and I said, "Absolutely!" He wanted to know if the groundhog had a name, and off the top of my head I said, "French Creek Freddie." Thus the legend of a competitor of Punxsutawney Phil was born. Skip had written a column for Groundhog Day, and it made the AP wire. On February 2, my phone rang off the hook, wanting to know what French Creek Freddie had predicted. I got calls from Maine, Florida, California, and several other states. Normally, I would stick strictly to biology, but Groundhog Day comes on February 2, a time when everyone needs a break and a little levity to counter the winter blahs. Since no one can define the difference between "six more weeks of winter" and an "early spring," the legend does no harm and might even generate some real interest in true biology. The whole allure of Groundhog Day is just for fun.

* * *

In the spring of 1976, another bison calf was born. This one was a bull calf. He had nursed, was walking around, and was healthy, but the mother had complications from giving birth and went down and died. We got as much colostrum milk as we could from the cow, collected the calf, and brought it over to a small pen behind the residence. I put the milk in a bottle with a nipple, warmed it, and sent a couple of the men to feed the calf. Shortly, they returned to my office saying they couldn't get the calf to eat. I took the bottle and said, "Come on. I'll show you how to force-feed it."

At the pen, the calf was backed into a corner, snorting and pawing the ground with his tail standing up. I went in intending to catch him and force him to take the bottle. When I got close, he tried to bolt past me along the fence. I caught him under the neck and reached across to grab the opposite flank. His momentum and weight (50–60 lbs.) caused my knuckles and elbows to buzz along the fence, removing a considerable amount of skin. After a protracted struggle, he was still refusing to eat, and I was dripping sweat and blood. I said, "To hell with this. He'll eat when he's hungry enough." I emptied the bottle into a water pan and exited the pen. As I closed the gate, I was startled to hear a loud slurping sound. He was drinking the milk from the pan. We did get him to take a bottle and, for a while, we kept him in a portable pen in a field behind the house. We named him Tennial. After all, he was a bison and it was 1976.

From the beginning, Tennial showed a decided preference for people over other animals. He loved to rub against you and have his neck and ears scratched. When he was weaned and on solid food, we moved him into the exhibit with the other bison. He wanted nothing to do with them and would patrol the exhibit fence where he could be closer to people. When he was almost a yearling (about 500 pounds with nubbins of horns emerging), John Weimer and I were in the bison exhibit working on a cow that needed some attention. I was observing the cow when Tennial came up behind me, hooked one small horn under my butt, and tossed me right over the hill. He only wanted attention, but I had had about enough. I started looking for a new home for him and found one at the Goode North American Zoo in Wheeling, WV. Before long, he wore out his welcome there. He derailed and upset their tweetsie railroad train and would just walk through about any fence that was between him and where he wanted to go. The last I heard of Tennial, he was about 1,500 pounds and had been shipped off to a bison ranch in Texas. I hope he finally learned that he was a bison and not a person.

* * *

A lady called me one morning and said that a large bird had landed in her yard and approached her three-year-old son who was terrorized and ran to the house screaming and crying. The bird followed him and was standing on the porch by the door. After some discussion, she said she would try to get it in a large cardboard box and bring it to the game farm. About an hour later, she showed up with a young brown pelican. How a pelican would appear in the forested mountains of West Virginia approximately 300 miles from its normal habitat, I could only guess. Perhaps some vacationer to the east coast had captured it and brought it home. It was obviously imprinted on people and would follow you around like a puppy wanting to be fed. Though it could fly, it chose not to, and it just hung around and followed whoever was walking around my office or the residence. We hoped that it would fly away on its own, but it did not. I actually learned to throw a cast net, just trying to keep it fed. It would consume astonishing amounts of fish, and the walkway between the house and my office soon became littered with white splotches of pelican poop. One of our summer employees was going to the beach with her family, so we boxed up the pelican and she took it to a wildlife refuge on the eastern shore. Once there, the pelican exhibited the same behavior it had with us, and they, in turn, sent it to a pelican rookery on an island in Florida. I hope it finally realized its true identity.

* * *

As our two daughters, Lori and Lisa, grew older and more responsible, they were included in the care and feeding of the young animals that appeared in our kitchen. One little animal that "pegs the cute meter" is a flying squirrel, and we had one that Lori wanted to keep in her bedroom. We fashioned a den for it from a three-pound coffee can with a warm bed, a water bottle holder, and small holes cut into the snap-on lid. She would feed the squirrel unsalted peanuts and sunflower seeds. She called him Freddie.

Just at daylight one morning, Lori burst into our bedroom exclaiming, "Freddie can fly! He can fly! He can really fly!"

Flying squirrels are nocturnal, and during the night, he had escaped from his den, scrambled up a curtain to the curtain rod, and launched himself across the room to the curtains on another window. He was repeating the process just for exercise. Lori was excited, I was amused, and Shelia was concerned about the curtains. Freddie got banned to a cage out in the shop.

* * *

Someone had brought us a crow which had been captured and made into a pet as a fledgling. We put it in an exhibit cage where it could fly around but could still be closely observed. That crow had an affinity for brightly colored or shiny objects and would grab those things and stash them around the inside of the cage.

On one occasion, a woman was poking at him with a five-dollar bill, folded lengthwise. He snatched the bill, flew up to his perch, and carefully tucked it into the foliage there. The woman squealed and turned to me, asking if I would get her money back. I said, "No, you just learned a five-dollar lesson to not pester the animals."

Over time, it was surprising to find the assortment of trinkets in that crow's cage—coins, marbles, costume jewelry, gum wrappers, etc.

Early one morning, I was on my way to the district office to make some copies. As I walked past the crow's cage, I very distinctly heard a woman's voice say "Hello, hello there!" There was no one around. It had to be the crow. Although he did that a few other times, we could never figure out what triggered him to talk.

* * *

The entrance to the game farm was at the intersection of routes four and twenty and the Alexander Road. Right at the corner, there was a deer pen of approximately one acre. The front of the pen faced routes four and twenty, and there was a concrete walkway along the front, metal pipe railing along the walkway, and a three-to-four-foot block wall down to parking space for five or six cars. There was a telephone booth on that lower level. We usually kept a buck and four or five does in that exhibit which had eight foot chain-link fence wired to steel posts around the perimeter. We always kept a big buck in that exhibit because that's what the public wanted to see. That fall, the buck in residence had big antlers, a large body, and a very aggressive attitude. He was dangerous, and he had absolutely no fear of people.

About one AM one night, Shelia elbowed me awake and said, "There's someone out by your office yelling something!"

I got up, went into the kitchen, and opened the window. There was a young man pacing back and forth by my office door yelling "Game Wardener! Game Wardener!"

I called out, "What's wrong?"

He said, "That big buck over there is out. Come and help us."

I quickly got dressed and went out with a big flashlight. Upon arriving at the pen, I could quickly see what had happened. There were four young men, all big, strapping lads and all quite drunk. They were driving a little Ford Pinto, had seen the big buck in the headlights as they turned on the Alexander Road, and decided to stop for a good look. The buck met them at the fence, and they probably kicked the fence to agitate him a little. He charged the fence, popped loose the tie wires, and suddenly he was free on their side of the fence. The buck wasn't going anywhere, as he had three of them "treed."

He was pacing back and forth in the parking area just daring them to come down to his level where he could attack. His ears were laid back, he was rolling his eyes, his hackles were up, and he was spoiling for a fight. One man was on top of the car, which had the doors open and the motor running; one was on top of the fence corner; one was on top of the phone booth; and the fourth had run to get help. I told the men that since they had caused the buck to get out, they would have to help me put him back in the pen. I went up on the walkway, unlocked the gate, and scuffed my feet to get the buck's attention. He came right over below me to accept the challenge, and I hooked one antler around one of the metal rail posts, and pushed back just enough to keep his attention. Then I told the men to each grab a leg and we'd half drag and half carry him back through the gate and turn him loose.

It took five of us to accomplish the task, and three or four minutes later, we released the buck back into the pen. Throughout the whole process, there was a great deal of laughing, yelling, and grunting and yelps of pain and a steady stream of profanity. The young men stayed until I had repaired the fence and then drove off still laughing and swearing. They had just had a great adventure that they're probably still talking about. For that matter, so am I.

* * *

One summer afternoon, paperwork had me at my desk in the office when a rusty and decrepit-looking VW van pulled into the driveway between the house and office and sputtered to a stop outside my office door. A rather disreputable-looking man with about five days' growth of white whiskers walked into my office and said, "Can I give you a lion?"

I said, "Do you have a lion?"

He said, "Yes."

I said, "Where is it?"

He said, "It's in the van."

I stepped out of the office and peered in through the window of the van. I was eyeball to eyeball with a full-grown male African lion. I was stunned. The lion was wearing a very heavy collar attached to a short length of heavy tow chain, which was attached to a heavy eyebolt in the center of the van floor. Everything that the cat could reach inside the van was totally destroyed. It looked like half a dozen hand grenades had exploded inside that van. I motioned the man back into my office and began to ask questions. He was very evasive about where he got the cat, how he had been keeping it, whether or not he had a decent facility to keep big cats or whether or not he was affiliated with any zoo or animal care facility. He did say that he had been feeding it chicken, he was out of money, and he was trying to find a home for the lion. I asked him to wait while I made some phone calls. I did get an encouraging response from the Cincinnati Zoo, which I told him about. I gave him some meat for the cat from our supply and twenty dollars for gas money. He started the van and drove away, heading for Cincinnati, I presume. I was so flabbergasted by the whole thing that I never did get his full name or the license plate number of his vehicle. I never heard anything about him or the lion again.

* * *

One of the most common "pets" that we received were raccoons. People would find a small raccoon and take it home for a pet. When it grew large enough to terrorize the family cat, maybe bite one of the kids, and open and trash every drawer or cabinet in the house, it was no longer so cute, and people would bring it to us. One woman brought in her pet raccoon, but she said she wanted to visit it every so often so that she would know it was all right. She made a nuisance of herself by showing up about twice a week to pet and cuddle "her baby."

One day, I heard people out in the shop, and I stepped out to see what was going on. This woman was there cuddling her baby "Bandit," kissing it on the mouth and letting it climb all over her.

When Bandit was back in his cage and the woman had gone, Theron came into the office and said, "Boy, that was close. I was cleaning Bandit's cage, and he was loose in the shop when I saw her coming. I just caught him and closed the cage door when she walked in."

I said, "Where was he?"

Theron said, "He was in the john playing in the commode!"

Little raccoons, as they grow and mature, can become incredibly adept at getting into mischief.
Photo by Steven Rotsch

* * *

One warm spring evening, the phone at the residence rang. When I answered, a nearly hysterical and very excited female voice said, "There's a bear on my porch, and if you don't do something about it, I'm going to shoot it." I managed to get her calmed down a little and got the particulars. Then I called Clyde and explained the situation and requested his help. Within a few minutes, Clyde arrived. I had my drug box and dart gun, and we loaded a big bear box into a pickup. Clyde knew where the woman's house was and we were on our way.

The woman who called was married to a young computer whiz. They were building a new house, and she was about eight months pregnant. The house was in a remote and isolated area, situated on a huge rock surrounded by forest with a dense understory of mountain laurel and rhododendron, and though they were living there, it was still unfinished, and some of the windows had not yet been installed. It had a small lawn and a sizable porch deck on the back side of the house. When we pulled into the yard, the lady met us on the deck by the back door.

She had heard a sound on the back porch. When she arrived at the door, which had an upper window, and flipped on the porch light, she was standing almost nose to nose with a very large black bear that was looking in through the window. The bear took off, and she ran to the phone to call me.

Clyde and I looked all around the house and found no sign of the bear except wet paw prints on the porch. However, we soon figured out what had happened. There was a large garbage bag on the porch that was almost half-full of watermelon rinds and an open fifty-pound bag of dog food under the porch. We explained that this was a "bear buffet," told them to secure the dog food, and offered to haul off the trash bag. With no easy food source, the bear probably wouldn't return. As we were preparing to leave, we were standing on the porch talking, and the lady suddenly pointed to the yard and exclaimed, "There he is!"

Coming across the yard was a very large black bear with a blue plastic tag in his left ear. That blue tag told us immediately that this bear had been in trouble before. I was thinking about the dart gun and the drug box.

I said, "Clyde, what do you think?'

He replied, "No problem. I'll just run him off."

Before I could say anything more, Clyde grabbed a broom that was standing by the door, jumped off the porch with a loud war whoop, and charged the bear. He whopped it on the rump at least three times before it blasted into the thick laurel. We waited for a little while, but the bear didn't come back. Ever! Clyde's method of solving the problem would never have occurred to me. I was as startled as the bear, and I was impressed!

Another time, also in early summer when young bears are searching for a new home range, we got a call requesting help to move a bear that had appeared in the Nitro/St. Albans area, a couple of suburbs of Charleston, the state capital. The call came at about 3:00 PM, and we were told that a helicopter would pick us up and take us to the site, so we should "get our equipment and be ready!" About forty-five minutes later, another call said the helicopter was down for repairs, and we'd have to drive. It was about a hundred miles to Nitro/St. Albans, and now we were racing the clock, as darkness would come at about 7:30 PM. We quickly loaded a bear box, the drug kit, and dart gun into a pickup and took off. I drove with Clyde riding shotgun and operating the radio. Most of the trip was on interstate highway, and we had communications with the state police, so I did not worry about speeding, and speed I did.

We arrived in Nitro at about 6:30 PM and were quickly directed to where the bear was last seen. One would have thought that Godzilla was destroying everything in the neighborhood. There were police cars, fire trucks, and EMT vehicles everywhere with all their lights flashing. People were standing along the streets, in their yards, and on their porches. Everyone was excited. This was better than a carnival! Clyde grabbed the dart gun, I grabbed the drug box, and we were off in pursuit of the bear. When we spotted him, we both estimated his size at one hundred to one hundred twenty-five pounds, and I loaded up a dart accordingly.

Many people think that all that is necessary to tranquilize an animal is to hit it with a dart, and it will immediately fall down in a deep sleep. They have seen too many Hollywood movies. In real life, it is necessary to have a good estimate of the animal's weight, a good hit with proper injection, and as much as five to ten minutes for the drug to take effect. This is not an exact procedure as there are many variables, and an animal can travel quite a distance in five to ten minutes.

In this case, an imperfect hit resulted in an improper injection and the pursuit of a groggy bear through backyards all over the neighborhood. It was getting dark. Finally, after two more darts, the bear was almost tranquilized in a backyard. It was trying to get over a stone wall when Clyde rushed in to grab and hold it until it went out, but it had enough strength to pull him over the wall where he landed on his head. The bear finally went out in the next backyard where we stuffed him into a box, loaded him in the pickup, and headed back to French Creek. It was now fully dark.

Clyde wanted to drive on the way back. I think he was more afraid of my speeding than he was of grabbing a woozy bear. He said, "You only hit the high spots on the way down here!"

A couple of days later, we released that bear in the Cranberry Backcountry.

CHAPTER XIV

Changes at French Creek

WHEN SHELIA AND I first moved to the game farm with two young daughters, there was already a long tradition of providing the public with information about the state's wildlife. This tradition was soon to be enhanced by the addition of a well-planned mobile wildlife exhibit.

The new exhibit had spaces for twelve small animal compartments, a dozen inanimate displays, two continuous loop slideshows with recorded sound, and was well lit so that it could be viewed after dark. It was moved by a strong truck that contained quarters for the operator, and it traveled with its own generator and water supply. It was available by request to fairs, festivals, and other public gatherings all over the state.

During the exhibit season (May through October), it was on the road almost every weekend, and it enabled us to provide wildlife information for thousands of West Virginians. It was interesting to note that the public's most frequently asked question was, "Where are the restrooms?" But it was encouraging to get insightful questions about food habits, range, habitat, reproduction, and life span. Lots of people really did want to know more about our native birds and animals.

Operating the mobile exhibit was a physically and emotionally demanding job, at entry-level pay, so many of the operators would transfer to another position after one season. Even so, we had a series of bright, well-educated, and hardworking young people who represented the DNR well for sixteen seasons and nearly 200,000 miles. The mobile exhibit was a success.

The mission of the DNR is to protect, manage, conserve, and manipulate the animals, fish, birds, and forests which belong to all citizens of the state for the maximum benefit of those citizens for the longest time possible. Since much of the money the DNR uses to operate comes from hunting and fishing license sales and taxes on sporting goods, I have always felt that one of the most important things we could do was to inform hunters and fishermen about what we're doing and why we're doing it. We must maintain rapport with the people who pay the bills. Therefore, in 1978, we decided to host a National Hunting and Fishing Day event at the game farm to recognize the contributions sportsmen make to conservation and to improve our relations with the public. The fourth weekend in September saw the grounds covered with exhibits, demonstrations, vendors, and public participation events. Over the years, attractions were added, and it continues to be a popular event.

Although we never stopped trying to make improvements at the game farm, sometimes progress could be dishearteningly slow. It was difficult to make an old facility attractive (sort of like putting lipstick on a pig). However, in 1984, monies from the Land and Water Conservation Fund of the US Department of Interior became available to us for planning and building completely new exhibits on another portion of the property. For almost two years, we were deeply involved with the details of construction, but finally, in September of 1986, the governor was on hand to dedicate the new facility and to rename it the West Virginia State Wildlife Center. It was no longer a "game farm." It was now an attractive destination where the public could observe, enjoy, and learn about the birds and animals of West Virginia.

The new facilities at the Wildlife Center quickly became a preferred destination for elementary school-field trips. In the spring, it was not uncommon to have a dozen or more school buses in the parking lot, and, as much as we could, we tried to provide each class with a tour guide who could help the children better understand our native birds and animals. There were a few points that I insisted must be made on each tour:

1. Never try to make a pet out of a wild animal, as you can never be sure how that animal will react in a given situation. There is never a happy ending to a pet wild animal story.

2. There are no animals that we cannot learn about, manage for, and keep and enjoy forever.

3. There are no "bad" animals (wolves) or "good" animals (bunnies). They are just animals that have been designed by nature over time to fit into a certain place in the total environment.

4. We all have a duty and responsibility to take good care of our environment, as we have the ability to control it and animals do not.

Sometimes it was very rewarding for us to see the "understanding light bulb" come on for these youngsters who had never before had animal biology explained to them in this way. Every animal that comes into this world is equipped to survive and reproduce to keep their species going. Not all of them succeed (remember the concept of population dynamics), but enough do to maintain the species unless the environment changes so drastically that they become extinct. The key phrase here is environmental change, so let's elaborate on those four points to gain a better understanding of wild animals.

1. On a December day, I received a call from a man who said he was a producer for *America's Most Wanted* (the TV show), and he wanted to know if we had a "trained buck deer." When I quit laughing, I explained that deer were not "trainable," but we did have a young buck that was unafraid of people. Why? He explained that they wanted

to film an episode that showed a primitive weapons hunter who was accused of killing his wife. When he described the scenario that he wanted to film, I told him that we could probably set up what he wanted.

The deer to be filmed had been an orphan bottle-fed fawn. He now had antlers. He was not afraid of people and was beginning to show some aggression. The film crew arrived—about a dozen city people from Los Angeles, New York, and Chicago who probably had little or no out-door experience—and I described the buck's behavior to them and warned them to get behind a tree if the buck approached them. We released the buck from a box in a naturally appearing woodlot where the "hunter/murder suspect" could stalk him and fire a shot with a black pow-der rifle (lots of smoke, but no bullet). The buck just stood there looking at us and chewing acorns. The producer asked if I could make him run at the shot. The second take, I picked up a stick and threw it at the buck at the shot. He laid his ears back and came for me. I dodged around a tree and grabbed his antlers to keep him off me. The game farm guys who were helping saw that I needed help and ran to assist. The buck started to pull back, and I thought he was trying to detach. I let go and he backed up and came at me again. That time, he punctured my hand with an antler tine. The guys arrived and we stuffed him back into the box. The camera crew was all worried that "Bambi" might be hurt while I was standing there with a punctured hand dripping blood. I went to the emergency room for treat-ment. The next morning, my infected hand looked like a boxing glove, and I spent the next five days in the hospital getting industrial strength antibiotics. The TV show aired, and the murderer was caught.

A week later, my supervisor who lived nearby called me and asked if the buck that got me had escaped, as a buck had just chased his neighbor back into his house. Could I bring a box or something to take care of it? I took "something," and, with no remorse, shot him in the neighbor's yard. He had become a menace.

It's important to note here that while many behaviors can be expected and predicted, they can often change very quickly. A case in point is the story of Kenny Hall and the mountain lion.

We had a young mountain lion that had been confiscated when it was just a kitten of six to eight pounds. It still had a mottled coat, and it was very playful. We kept it in the shop where the guys would let it out of its cage to explore the shop and romp and play. It grew quickly and soon became large enough to inflict pain and even cause bleeding when tussling with the men. It was very tame and seemed to enjoy being petted and having its ears and chin scratched. It wasn't long before we felt it was big enough to be introduced to the mountain lion exhibit for display to the public.

Kenny Hall was a young conservation aide on our staff. He was a local farm boy, twenty-six years old, strong and work hardened, and quite familiar with the potential hazards of working with large animals. He arrived early for work one Saturday morning and decided to make a quick tour of the exhibit loop to check for any problems. He discovered one in the mountain lion exhibit. That enclosure had a fourteen-foot-high-chain-link fence with electrified wire at the top, and one of the insulators was shorted out and snapping. Kenny went and got an extension ladder, set it up in the back of a pickup truck, and climbed it to repair the snapping insulator. As he worked on the insulator with his elbow across the top of the fence, he was shocked and surprised to suddenly have the young mountain lion clamp on to his arm. Of course, it hurt, and the immediate response was to punch the cat in the nose. Instantly, it was "game on" for the cat, and play went to attack in a nanosecond. In a few seconds, the encounter ended and the mountain lion was not hurt, but Kenny sustained injuries that kept him in the hospital for nearly two weeks, required two sessions of very involved and delicate surgery, and prevented him from working for nearly four months. We soon declawed that cat, and I kept the claws and gave them to Kenny when he was able to return to work.

Even though the mountain lion was acclimated to people and seemed very tame, there was no overcoming the power of the preprograming in the DNA. There is never a happy ending to a pet wild animal story.

I frequently explained to school groups that wild animal behavior is preprogramed by a complex molecule called DNA, and it works much like their computers do in schools. The problem is that none of the keys are marked, and we don't know which key or keys will prompt what reaction. In that buck's or lion's cases, absence of fear prompted him to respond to humans in the same way he would have to an adversary. His natural environment had changed, but he could not change with it.

Kenny Hall, who was injured by a mountain lion, presents an unwilling French Creek Freddie on a cold February 2 morning.
Photo by Steven Rotsch

2. It has been said that "we grow too soon old and too late smart," and this certainly applies to humans all over the world, but let's narrow that down a bit and take a look at North America.

    The indigenous people who had lived here for centuries had worked out lifestyles that harmonized with nature. Although they did impact the environment, their influence was minimal because most of them considered themselves to be part of it. They attempted to live within the environment, not dominate it. Enter immigrants from "more advanced and civilized" parts of the world, and exploitation began. That was accelerated by the industrial revolution, and the mad dash for profits took over, almost always with complete disregard for the environment.

    Vast forests, which served as filters, were cut down and made into lumber or just burned to clear the land. The cleared land was subjected to the same crops year after year until the soil was depleted and fallow. Streams were choked with debris and silt from runoff. But no matter, we could always just move west where there was always fertile land and more forest. It took nearly 200 years for us to finally wake up and realize what we were doing to our environment. For many species of wildlife, it was too late. They were gone forever. We may never know exactly how many species have become extinct, but we frequently refer to one glaring example: the passenger pigeon. It was discovered too late that a certain level of social stress was necessary for successful reproduction. We had so altered the environment that the stress threshold could not be met, and the passenger pigeon became extinct. Many other species became extinct, endangered, or threatened because they could no longer survive and reproduce in their original range.

    About the end of the nineteenth and beginning of the twentieth century, a new science began to emerge and grow: the science of wildlife biology. The basic premise of wildlife biology is actually pretty simple. If we can discover the requirements of a species, we can manipulate the environment to provide those necessities and thereby ensure the survival of that species.

That seems pretty straightforward, but as they say, "the devil is in the details." To "discover the requirements" can be an extremely complicated task, as we must learn about many aspects of an animal's life: range, food habits, distribution, physiology, breeding behavior, social behavior, preferred habitat, nutritional needs, relationships with other species and on and on. Assembling all this information is time-consuming and usually expensive; therefore much of the research has been aimed at popular game species such as deer, elk, game birds, waterfowl, and small game (rabbits, squirrels, etc.). Much of the funding for research and management has come from sportsmen and women who buy licenses and pay taxes to ensure that their preferred species do not become threatened or endangered. Sometimes it is possible to successfully manage for a species that is not fully understood, and that management frequently benefits many other species. And so the research must continue to learn all we can about how a particular species fits into the total environment.

3.   Frequently, in the course of conducting a school tour, as we were approaching the wolf enclosure, I would hear mutterings about the "big bad wolf." I would stop and ask the group, "How many of you think there are bad animals?" Several hands would go up, and I'd ask for examples. The responses were usually "wolves, snakes, skunks, or chicken hawks." Then I'd ask for examples of good animals, and the response would be "bunnies, deer, songbirds, or squirrels." I would then explain that there are no "good" or "bad" animals. Each animal has a contribution to make that helps maintain the incredibly complex balance of nature. Predators (animals that eat other animals) help control the numbers of herbivores (animals that eat plants) so that they

don't destroy the vegetation. Herbivores provide food for predators and help keep vegetation in check. Every animal in every environment has a specific role to play, and that role will affect almost every animal or plant in that environment in some way. Although the role of a single species is fairly limited in scope, when taken together, the roles of all the species of animals and plants that make up the environment are so interrelated and incredibly complex that the most sophisticated creations of man look like 1 + 1 = 2.

4. Genesis 1:26 says, "And God said, Let us make man in our image, after our likeness: and let them have dominion over the fish of the sea, and over the fowl of the air, and over the cattle, and over all the earth, and over every creeping thing that creepeth upon the earth." Unfortunately, the Bible doesn't give us an owner's manual or a service schedule for this wonderful gift of earth that we control. We just have to muddle along on our own and hope for the best. Most people would agree that a very valuable gift should be cherished and cared for, but in practice we've exhibited ignorance, apathy, indifference, self-interest, and greed in the ways we've treated our environment. We have timbered, plowed, mined, drilled, dredged, and built over much of North America. As Pete Seeger sang in the 1960s, "we've paved paradise and put up a parking lot."

If this book serves no other purpose, I hope it will cause some people to pause and think before they barge into some project that will alter the environment we pass on to future generations. I hope that my great-great-grandchildren will be able to also marvel at the sounds of woodpeckers, spring peepers, bugling elk, and migrating geese.

CHAPTER XV

Rumors, Misinformation, Observations

I HAVE COME to the belief that a rumor has at least ten times the half-life of the cold, hard truth. I have also come to the conclusion that one of the most difficult tasks a man can undertake is to get other people to think and to think objectively.

A case in point is a rumor that began more than twenty years ago. The rumor was that the WV DNR was flying around the state dropping rattlesnakes from helicopters to help control the wild turkey population. Now a thinking person would immediately start asking questions: Why? Does the turkey population need to be controlled? Where do the rattlesnakes come from? Do rattlesnakes really have an effect on turkey populations? How much do helicopter hours cost? Can the snakes survive the fall uninjured? If there is an over-population problem, why not just extend the seasons or increase the bag limit? Isn't it the DNR's mission to provide maximum recreational opportunities for license buyers? The answers are of course obvious! A thinking person will quickly come to the conclusion that the rumor is pure rubbish. And yet the rumor still persists! Just last fall, I was having breakfast when a hunter approached me and asked if the rumor was true, having heard from the waitress that I was a retired DNR biologist. He received the "thinking lecture" and was satisfied and thanked me for enlightening him. I was flabbergasted.

Another rumor was that the DNR had imported and introduced coyotes into West Virginia (reason not stated). We did not! The facts are that coyotes found their own way into the state because they are intelligent, adaptable, and were able to colonize a habitat where competing predators (wolves, mountain lions) were no longer present. Given the high populations of deer, wild turkeys, and small animals, the coyotes found the new habitat to their liking and made themselves at home. It is important to note here that predator populations are dependent on the populations of prey species, not the other way around. If predators cannot find enough to eat, they cannot survive and reproduce. Before long, the ratio of predators to prey will reach an equilibrium and stabilize with a predator-prey ratio that is sustainable.

It is not sound biology to blame predators alone for reducing numbers of species that we wish to exploit. Instead, let's do some objective thinking for ourselves. Are the numbers of our preferred species really declining? Is the habitat for our preferred species changing, or has it remained stable? What other factors would cause a decline (overharvesting, predation, less available food and cover, disease, parasites, exceptionally severe weather)? Or could the decline be caused by a combination of these factors? Most likely it comes down to a combination of factors, and all of these need to be addressed to restore a population to abundance.

Yes, coyotes do prey on deer, but they are not the only factor controlling deer populations, and other factors must be considered.

Another widely believed bit of misinformation circulated around the state was that West Virginia was home to a wild, free-ranging population of mountain lions. I suppose that misconception is understandable because after all, a common moniker for the state is "Wild, Wonderful West Virginia." I'm sure there are plenty of people who would like to think that the state is still wild enough to support mountain lions. I don't think so, and here's why.

Mountain lions are pretty large animals, commonly weighing from ninety to one hundred fifty or more pounds. Animals that size must leave some evidence of their presence (tracks, scat, loose hairs on thorns or fences, dens or sleeping areas, remains of a kill, territorial marking sites such as scratching posts or scent posts). No such evidence has been found and verified. DNR biologists, myself included, have investigated mountain lion sightings and reports many times without finding any tangible evidence of the big cats. Many of the reports were extremely vague as in "My cousin's husband was coming home after a midnight shift last Thursday, and a mountain lion ran across the road in front of him just before he got to Pickens." Of course, that was too vague to follow, but the cousin's husband told plenty of people who were eager to pass the story along.

West Virginia has plenty of rough and tumble outdoorsmen who like to pursue raccoons, bobcats, foxes, and bears with hounds. Mountain lions are not marathon runners and, when pursued by dogs, will usually tree pretty quickly. All these hunters with hounds have not treed a mountain lion.

Mountain lions are extremely susceptible to feline distemper and will often die within twenty-four hours of contracting the disease. It is very likely that a free-ranging mountain lion would, at some point, come in contact with common house cats or feral house cats which are notorious carriers of the disease. Mountain lions would not survive long in this environment.

* * *

During deer season in West Virginia, most of the state's forests are penetrated by hunters carrying high-powered rifles. It is hard to imagine that a deer hunter with a chance to shoot a mountain lion would not do so. That has not happened!

Now, with all that being said, I received a call one day that a farmer in Pendleton County had shot and killed a mountain lion that had killed and was eating one of his sheep. A conservation officer was bringing the cat to me for examination. A couple of hours later, the officer arrived with a young mountain lion that had been shot through the chest and eviscerated by the farmer. The entrails were in a big plastic bag. I quickly refrigerated the cat and the bag and began making phone calls to solicit information.

The next morning, I received another call that the same farmer had lost another sheep to a mountain lion and that two of our biologists were on their way to capture it. Later that evening, I met the other biologists who transferred another mountain lion into my truck (in a deer-sized crate), and I returned to French Creek and released this one into a holding pen. Quickly, this whole episode was becoming too coincidental to believe. Both cats were not yet mature (about sixty to sixty-five pounds). The dead cat appeared normal, but the live one was missing about two thirds of its tail. The live cat had killed a sheep and dragged it into a corner of an old rail fence where it remained for more than three hours with several people watching it from only about thirty yards away. It made no attempt to flee even when the tranquilizer dart hit it. This was certainly not normal behavior.

I was able to speak with Dr. Frank Hayes of the Southeast Wildlife Disease Study Group. I explained the whole situation to him, and he asked me to send him the entrails from the dead cat and fecal samples from the live one, which I did as quickly as possible. A few days later, Dr. Hayes called to report what he'd discovered. He gave me the scientific names of two parasites that he'd found in both cats. One parasite is common only in Florida, the other is common only in animals in captivity. He also explained that big cats in captivity will sometimes damage an extremity when biting off the umbilical cord of a newborn. This is caused by stress and anxiety. It might explain the stub tail. When I asked for his conclusion, his opinion was that the two cats were probably born and weaned in captivity in Florida and later released where someone thought it was suitably wild for mountain lions.

Because there are misguided animal lovers who think a wild animal would make a good pet, they will sometimes purchase a young mountain lion or bear cub (on the black market or illegally) and take it home for the kids. They quickly discover that the animal is not only unsuitable but also potentially dangerous. At that point, they will search out a remote area in the state and release the now problem animal to fend for itself. For that reason, I would not declare that a "sighting" is false, but I do not believe that an unequipped released animal will survive long enough to mature and reproduce.

I suppose that rumors have a place in the human psyche, but until there is positive proof, I will remain skeptical of stories about mountain lions in West Virginia, Bigfoot, Sasquatch, Lizard Man, and the Loch Ness Monster.

Finally, one time, a gentleman approached me with a question. "I don't think West Virginia has many mountain lions anymore, do we?"

I replied, "No, Sir. I don't think so."

He said, "Just as I thought! I don't see nearly as many of 'em as I used to!"

Another common misconception is that "we need to import some of those big northern whitetails to stimulate hybrid vigor in our deer herd, and we'll be able to kill bigger bucks." That will not work. There is a principal in mammalogy called Bergmann's rule that states that within a species, larger individuals are found in colder climates and smaller individuals are found in warmer climates. The idea behind this "rule" is that larger animals lose less heat. Conversely, smaller animals can allow more heat to dissipate. This allows deer to survive very cold conditions in the North and very hot conditions in the South. West Virginia lies about halfway between Florida Key deer (adults of about fifty pounds) and Maine white-tails (adults of up to three hundred pounds), so we should not be surprised that our deer are about one hundred fifty to one hundred sixty pounds as adults. Nature has genetically equipped deer to fit their environment.

Most people who are interested in deer know that at least three factors must be favorable for deer to reach their maximum potential. Genetics (the blueprint for size, general health, and physical characteristics), nutrition (the amount and quality of food), and time (deer seldom reach the age of seven to eight years) are necessary for a buck to reach trophy status. In the wild, a seven-to-eight-year-old buck is rare. That's why it is considered a trophy.

Many times, conclusions about wildlife are reached because of personal observations. Sometimes these conclusions are accurate, but many times they are not because all the factors impacting the subject have not been considered. It is irresponsible to blame predators for the decline in a local deer herd while ignoring the fact that prime habitat has "grown out" and can no longer support as many deer. Personal observations are important, but don't hang your hat on them until they've been verified by multiple sources.

CHAPTER XVI

Behavior

WHEN I WAS about sixteen or seventeen, we lived on a small farm on the edge of town. Dad kept five or six cows that he milked by hand for our family's use, and we sold the extra milk. He milked, and my job was to feed and water the cows, refresh their bedding, and clean out the cement trough behind the cows where the manure and straw accumulated. This was later spread on the fields for fertilizer.

One day, I was shoveling out the trough behind the cows when one of them lashed out with a back leg that hit me in the thigh and dumped me in the trough in the manure. I was so angry that I popped up and hit her with my fist as hard as I could five or six times on the hip. To my amazement, she dropped to her knees and began to eat hay. Her head was enclosed in a stanchion, and she could neither flee nor fight back. Her reaction was to do something totally unrelated to the current situation, and maybe that situation would go away. This behavior is called a displacement reaction. I have been interested in animal behavior ever since.

Let's look at the basics. If you can't survive, you can't reproduce. If you can't reproduce, the species can't survive and will become extinct. There are myriads of behavior which are geared to ensure survival. Sight, smell, hearing, communication, and habits all combine to help an animal find food, avoid danger, and live in an environment that is as stress-free as possible. Young animals learn from adults about where to find food, safe bedding and resting areas, easier trails, and sources of danger to be avoided. They learn that the alarm cries of other species may signal danger to themselves. They learn that the communications of their own species may indicate food, danger, or safety. Within a species, body language is usually quite important, and most animals are more attuned to it than many people would suspect.

Since white-tailed deer are so popular and well studied, let's take a look at some of their behavior and means of communications. A slow walk with the head out in front, ears moving slowly and randomly, and an occasional short sideways flip of the tail will indicate to other deer that food is available and things are relatively safe. A rigid upright posture with head up and eyes and ears focused in one direction indicates that something is amiss. The stomp of a front foot or a loud snort indicates that a source of danger has been located. This is usually quickly followed by full-out flight with erect white tails waving from side to side to warn all other deer in the vicinity. Areas where deer bed down will almost always have certain characteristics: quick escape routes, cover to camouflage outlines, advantageous breezes to carry scent, and good lines of sight where deer can detect movements around them. Any time two or more deer are bedded together, they will be separated by some space and they will be facing in different directions to allow them to scan 360 degrees around them. Deer have incredible senses of smell and hearing, and though they are color blind, they usually detect the slightest bit of motion. Deer are creatures of habit, and, unless serious changes happen in their environment, will frequent the same areas to feed, bed down, and travel just as previous generations have done. You could say that these behaviors are instinctual or inherited or learned from mature deer, and you'd be correct. After all, behaviors that enhance survival are what evolution is all about. It's interesting to note here that danger to an individual deer (predators like wolves, bears, bobcats, mountain lions, and even man) almost always came from ground level. The result was that deer's attention was focused there and they seldom looked up. With the advent of modern archery, hunters have been taking advantage of that trait by hunting from elevated tree stands. With the use of tree stands come additional sounds, scent, and movement. I have noticed that more deer seem to be glancing up and becoming alerted by out-of-place blobs in the trees. Is it possible that I'm seeing the evolution of a change of behavior?

Volumes have been written on deer behavior, and the subtle and obscure nuances of survival, social, and reproductive behaviors of deer are beyond the scope of this book. Suffice it to say that the study of deer behavior can be a lifelong pursuit, and we still won't know all we'd like to.

All other animals have behaviors that are characteristic of their species, and each one is fascinating in its own right. I would be remiss if I didn't include at least a few.

* * *

When outlaws robbed the stagecoach, they grabbed the strong-box and "hightailed" it for the hills. The deputy marshal "played possum" on the sidewalk until the shooting stopped. He "bristled" when the cattle rancher insulted his sheep. The whole family "worked like beavers" to get the sod house ready for winter. Old "Hawkeye" was first to spot the cavalry coming to the rescue. She "barked" at him when he spilled flour on the floor, but she didn't "raise a stink" over it. After he "flew the coop," the outlaw was "slippery as an eel," but they finally caught him and he "sang like a mockingbird." These and many other Old West terms and sayings all have their origins in characteristic animal behavior.

Hightailing it—Many species of animals, especially prey species, will flee danger with their tails carried straight up in the air. This behavior may prevent a predator such as a wolf from grabbing the tail and holding on to slow down escape and allow other wolves to join in. It may also serve to confuse a predator about where to strike, and it could allow more flight speed by not getting in the way of flying feet. Examples of hightailing animals would include bison, deer, and even chipmunks.

Playing possum—Most people are familiar with the phrase, but not many have actually witnessed the behavior. An opossum, when caught by a predator, can achieve a catatonic state, resembling death. It will lie on its side with its tongue hanging out of its open mouth, eyes closed, and heart rate reduced. If the predator loses focus or interest, the opossum can recover quickly and escape by climbing.

Bristled—The behavior of a porcupine when it is threatened is to pull its four feet close together and erect its quills (modified hairs) to point outwards. The quills are stiff and sharp and can inflict painful injuries to an aggressor. Porcupines are not aggressive but this bristled behavior is a very good defensive measure.

Worked like beavers—Beavers are very industrious in their efforts to control their environment. They build houses of sticks and mud and use these same materials to create dams to hold back water. Water is essential for beaver survival because they are excellent swimmers and quite at home in the water, but they are slow and ungainly on dry land and subject to predation. As long as they can remain in or very near water, they are safe, but when food (sticks, branches, and bark) near water is exhausted, they are subject to predation, and the beaver colony will have to move on until that area regrows woody vegetation. Beavers can alter their environment, but they cannot completely control it. A beaver colony is always busy moving sticks and mud to raise or maintain a safe water level.

Hawk eye or eagle eye—Birds of prey (hawks, eagles, owls) are renowned for their exceptional vision. A hawk can spot prey as small as a mouse or vole on the ground among vegetation from a hundred feet or more in the air. It's no wonder then that a person who has exceptional vision was often nicknamed hawk eye or eagle eye.

Barked—A squirrel that spots unusual movement in the forest will emit a quick and explosive chatter to announce the presence of danger to other woodland inhabitants. This barking is usually accompanied by quick movements to gain a better vantage point and rapid jerking of the tail. It is an insistent scolding sound that attracts attention and puts other animals on alert.

Raise a Stink—When a skunk is threatened with danger, it will assume a posture with its tail raised high in the air. Then, while maintaining the posture, it will perform a little foot stomping dance of warning. If an attack is pressed, the skunk will spray scent into the face of the attacker (it can do this over a one hundred eighty-degree radius), causing temporary blindness and a terrible odor along with loss of smell. If the warning dance works and the aggressor backs away, the skunk will amble along on its way. We all know it's best to conserve ammunition and not raise a stink.

Flew the coop—Any animal or bird that has successfully escaped from captivity is said to have flown the coop. This is a common phrase that describes the loss of poultry or pigeons but is also used to describe animals that have escaped.

Slippery as an eel—If you have ever tried to hold a live eel, you'll understand the term. If you haven't, an eel is muscular, in constant motion, very slick, and just about impossible to hold on to.

Sang like a mockingbird—The mockingbird is a medium-sized gray songbird with white markings (chevrons) on the wings. It feeds on insects that move when the bird flashes the white chevrons by quickly extending the wings. Mockingbirds are prolific singers, but the most interesting thing about them is that they sing not only their own songs but also the songs of other bird species around them. It is important to understand that birds do not sing because they are happy, because they enjoy the sounds of music, or because they feel a need to express themselves. They sing to define their territory to others of their own and other species. They sing to attract mates. They sing to communicate. In other words, they sing to survive and to reproduce. Bird songs are serious business. For a mockingbird, this is very serious business. By singing the songs of other species, the mockingbird may dissuade thrushes, robins, wrens, and others that compete for food from entering his territory thereby increasing his chances of survival for himself and his family. To sing like a mockingbird is to tell the truth part of the time and to make up fibs part of the time.

Most young animals seem to be blessed with excess energy. This energy is expended in activities like running, jumping, snooping, tussling with peers, exploring, and tasting. We call this activity "play." Actually, this activity is the beginning of survival training for adulthood. As animals grow older and more mature, the play activities decrease and the serious activities of survival and reproduction take over.

Let's pause here for a quick biology lesson. Every cell in the body of every living organism contains deoxyribonucleic acid (DNA). This is the self-replicating material that passes on hereditary traits from one generation to the next. The information is encoded in the sequencing of four chemical bases: adenine (A), guanine (G), cytosine (C), and thymine (T). When you talk about humans sharing DNA with each other and with other animals, you're talking about this sequencing pattern because all DNA contains the same four chemical bases. We know that 99.99% of the genetic information in DNA is common to all humans. The remaining 0.01% is responsible for differences in eye, skin and hair color, height, and resistance to certain diseases, etc. We also know that we share a great deal of our DNA sequencing with other animals, insects, and even plants. This sharing of DNA sequencing can be as high as 98.7% (chimpanzees) to 50–60% (bananas). Given this background information, it should come as no surprise that there are similarities of behavior between humans and animals.

Several examples come quickly to mind. Fear (or fright) is nearly universal among animals and people. Anger is a common trait as are maternal instinct, desire to be dominant, aggressiveness for food, submission to dominance, indifference to stimuli which do not directly affect us, and willingness to go along with the crowd (herd mentality). These and many other behaviors are easy to recognize in both animals and humans. Because of these behavioral similarities, some people have come to the conclusion that if animal behavior is so similar to that of humans, then we must be equal. This type of thinking has led to a term called anthropomorphism.

CHAPTER XVII

Anthropomorphism

I'M NOT SURE when it might have started, perhaps with cavemen trying to domesticate wolves into hunting partners or with the advent of animated cartoons featuring talking animals, but a phenomenon has emerged called anthropomorphism. It is the attributing of human characteristics to animals. These would include the ability to talk, to plan and scheme, to be embarrassed, to worry, to manipulate situations, to express love and loyalty, to grieve, to deceive, and so on. Many of these characteristics can be observed in animals that have been domesticated because many generations have been selectively bred to produce animals whose behavior is acceptable to humans. Not only has the DNA programming been altered, but long association has resulted in some human behavior rubbing off on them. There are many, many examples of animal behavior that seem surprisingly human, especially those with which we form a strong bond such as dogs and horses, but keep in mind that dogs, horses, and other animals have lived and worked together with people for thousands of years.

Wild animals are a whole different ball game. They have been designed and shaped to fit into a narrow slot in the overall environment where their existence and behavior contribute to the incredibly complex ecology. At some point, whether they are predators, prey, or scavengers, nature will recycle them to provide for other animals or plants. In the meantime, their purpose in life is to survive, reproduce, and keep their slot filled to make their contribution to the ecology. There it is again! A simple concept: survive and reproduce. It is vital to all wild animals.

For nearly 300 years (an instant in geologic time), change has been happening in North America and around the world. The pace of change continues to accelerate rapidly. Ideas that were science fiction only a few years ago are becoming outmoded today. As proliferating technology draws us farther and farther away from basic biology, we begin to lose our concern for the production of food and the natural quality of our environment. (Someone else will take care of it.) And yet thousands of years of close association with nature cannot be erased in a few decades, and we retain an affinity for flora and fauna. We feel a need to express that affinity in some way, and it often takes the form of anthropomorphism. Unfortunately, we tend to pick and choose individual animals that we like or that we find attractive and ignore almost everything else. We throw ourselves into these causes and frequently expend a lot of time, effort, and ridiculous amounts of money to briefly extend the life of an individual animal that will never contribute to its species. We do this because it makes us feel good, and we congratulate ourselves. This is commendable for animals that are threatened or endangered, but for those species that are not, wouldn't it be better to support research or habitat management to benefit the species?

While manning the mobile wildlife exhibit at public gatherings, I have been confronted by people who have obviously been afflicted with severe cases of anthropomorphism.

"How can you be so cruel to keep these poor little animals in those small cages for people to look at? Don't you think these animals would rather be wild and free?"

I explained, "We feel that the sacrifice of the freedom of these few animals is well worth it if people can see them, learn about them, and become more solicitous of the welfare of the species in the future." Those confrontations have stuck with me for many years, and I have pondered the dialogue hundreds of times. The simple answer to the question "Don't you think these animals would rather be wild and free?" is no because wild animals are not capable of analyzing the differences between hypothetical scenarios. Animals do not think in abstract terms. They live in the here and now, and they employ the attributes they have to fulfill their mandate to survive and reproduce.

What troubles me the most about these encounters is that someone who probably has no training about life cycles, habitat, carrying capacity, or population dynamics can be so aggressively obnoxious when you fail to embrace their views. I have met several of these people, and for years, I have wondered how they become so emotional, so intractable, and so unwilling to think. I have seen people aggressively advocate for wolves in Isle Royale National Park, for wolves and grizzly bears in Yellowstone National Park, and for the protection of mountain lions in California. "Let them be wild and free!" "Let nature take its course!" are the rallying cries from these advocates. But when the subject switches to less glamorous species like ants, ticks, spiders, mosquitoes, lice, rats, bats, snakes, cockroaches, coyotes, and even feral swine, the advocates and their rallying cries disappear. Why? Because it is now time for a healthy dose of realism.

People are animals, too, and we share a lot of characteristics with other animals, but we also have characteristics that are unique in the animal kingdom. We can reason, we can compare, we can consider abstract ideas. We have harnessed fire, invented the wheel, made steel, developed religion, produced art, music, and poetry, established worldwide instant communications, learned to fly, and sent men to the moon and back. We have the ability to completely control our environment. No other animal has ever had the ability to do those things.

The Bible tells us that we are created in God's image and that we have dominion over all living things on the earth. History has proved the dominion part, but the "God's image" part remains in question because we still haven't mastered the stewardship and responsibility toward life on earth that God's image implies.

There is no doubt that the earth, with all its flora and fauna, was created and didn't just happen randomly. The same four components of DNA exist in all life, and at least some DNA is shared by all life. We have only just begun to understand the intricate interrelationships of our flora and fauna. Succumbing to anthropomorphism will only distort or slow down our understanding. We must remember to tell ourselves that owls don't talk to rabbits à la the *Bambi* movie. Owls kill and eat rabbits. That's the way God made them.

So let's be realistic. Nature is not warm and fuzzy, is not influenced by "cute," is not emotional, does not show favoritism, and does not relent when conditions become severe. Stewardship then is recognizing the ways of nature and manipulating them for the benefit of those species which are assets to mankind and controlling those species which are detrimental. The responsibility part of the equation lies in the fact that all life on earth is important, and to allow any life form to disappear or become extinct might be forgoing a chance to cure cancer, prevent Alzheimer's, eliminate diabetes, slow the human aging process, prevent heart disease, etc.

It is time for us to accept and objectively execute the role of the dominant species on earth.

CHAPTER XVIII

Retirement

I<small>T WAS A</small> couple of days before Christmas some years ago and the kids had gone to bed. Shelia and I had wrapped a few presents when I suddenly realized that I had not yet fed my dogs. I hurried and got some dog food, pulled on a coat, and headed for the kennel behind the house. It had snowed that day, and there were five or six inches of fresh snow on the ground. About halfway to the kennel, I became aware that it was very quiet. I stopped and stood listening for several minutes. There was no sound. As I stood there surrounded by and absorbed in total silence, I looked up and saw a few stars twinkling through the clouds and a few snowflakes falling straight down. It was a magical moment, and I offered up a prayer of thanks for the silence, for my family, and for a lifestyle and job that I dearly loved. It occurred to me that many of my experiences were unique and that someday I should write about them. I even came up with a title. I'm sorry that it took so long, as I'm sure some of my memories have faded.

A few years after that incident, I had a chance to revisit an area that I had been quite familiar with as a boy. It was a cove on a hillside right below where the old sawmill stood. I'd go with Dad and watch him cut and haul logs to that mill with a team of horses. It was a great place for a boy to explore and spend time. I remembered the cove well. The cove was about twenty-five acres and extended from a small creek to a ridgeline, about one-fourth mile away and two hundred feet higher. There were saplings and small trees around the perimeter, and the center was about twelve to fifteen acres of meadow complete with fences and several haystacks.

I walked along the ridgeline to the old mill site and found no trace that a sawmill had ever been there. I descended toward the center of the cove and found myself in a solid canopy forest. I was taken aback, realizing that well within the span of one man's lifetime, nature had reclaimed this ground. It gives me comfort to realize that given enough time, nature is strong and resilient enough to erase most of the damage done by mankind.

Great civilizations have risen and fallen in the many centuries of mankind's history. For many of these, we still don't know what caused their rise or their fall, but we do know that nature has reclaimed many of the areas where they occurred. It's obvious that change is inexorable and unrelenting.

My hope at this point is that mankind will not rush into the future so recklessly and heedlessly that we ignore nature and cause more damage to the earth than nature can heal. Perhaps we can learn to live in harmony with nature and stop trying to beat it into submission.

Though it was never written into my job description, there was one principle that I always followed. Perhaps I could say or do something that would stimulate others to notice, appreciate, respect, and maybe even work to improve our environment.

The time came when circumstances made
retirement look like a pretty good option.
Photo by Steven Rotsch

If you were to ask any wildlife biologist if they chose their career because of the money, I'm sure you'd get a derisive laugh and a comment like "Hardly!" or "You've got to be kidding!" People choose wildlife careers because they love the outdoors, they are fascinated by animals, they don't mind either intellectual or physical hard work, or because they believe their efforts can make a difference.

I was fortunate to work with many professionals who were bright, innovative, dedicated, and hardworking. I'm proud to say that in West Virginia, most of the wildlife management decisions, as well as rules and regulations, were made because there was a sound biological basis for them.

West Virginia is a beautiful state blessed with good people, wonderful scenery, and abundant natural resources. Hunting, fishing, hiking, skiing, white water rafting, and other outdoor activities make the whole state a natural playground. Spend a few days in West Virginia, and you'll soon understand why it's called wild and wonderful.

In a thirty-two-year career, I never had a single day when I got up in the morning and said to myself, "Man, I hate to go to work today." I've never met another man who could say that!

I am grateful.

Bill Vanscoy

ABOUT THE AUTHOR

BILL VANSCOY IS a lifelong outdoor enthusiast. In addition to a career as a wildlife biologist, he has been involved with several conservation organizations, such as Ducks Unlimited, Ruffed Grouse Society, Wild Turkey Federation, and Rocky Mountain Elk Foundation. He still hunts and fishes and enjoys reading. He now lives with his wife, Shelia, in the Santee Cooper area in South Carolina.

CPSIA information can be obtained
at www.ICGtesting.com
Printed in the USA
LVHW070205090521
686901LV00023B/1240